MW01633382

KALEB SETH PERL

OPERATION: Human Freedom

A REVOLUTION IN HUMAN BECOMING

VOL.3

NEW REVOLUTIONS PUBLISHING

Published by New Revolutions Publishing

ISBN-13: 978-1-9162613-7-2 (paperback)
First published: 2020

Cover Concept: Kaleb Seth Perl & Rebekah Yael Nur

Cover Design & Book Formatting: Rebekah Yael Nur

Contact: ksperl@protonmail.com

Due to the nature of the contents of the books in the 'Revolution in Human Becoming' series, it would be of most benefit to the reader to have read the previous two volumes in this series: Vol. 1 - *Tyranny Against Human Consciousness*; Vol 2 - *Welcome to the Machine*.

This is not a commercial consideration - it is a functional one. Each volume in this series provides a stepping-stone to the next - both in terms of material and immaterial resources.

This is a suggestion only, and for the reader's consideration.

CONTENTS

INTRODUCTION

'There are three classes of people: those who see;
those who see when they are shown;
those who do not see.'

Leonardo da Vinci

The freedom to be human is about the responsibility to make freewill choices. Those choices can be made. They should be made – yet from your *own minds*, not from the influence of others. There can be no freedom for the individual if there is no freedom to think for oneself. This is the difference between being a player and a puppet. The choice to act from one's own sense of self is what will determine the type of future that exists for the human species on this planet. If you do not take *real choice* into your own hands, then you are no better than being a colony planet. If you exist through the control and manipulation of external influences then you are a slaveforce, not an independent sentient species. This is a critical and urgent decision in the crossroads you are upon collectively.

The choice is to actively use your conscious will and intention, or to give your responsibility for living over to others. If you are unable to create the necessity for the conditions to evolve your gills into lungs, you shall not be equipped to leave the fishbowl to breath the air. The capacity to leave behind your current state and to evolve into a new future for the human being rests with you. You shall not be brought, dragged, into a new life. You have to arrive so that you can be met.

These messages are about that possibility.

PART ONE

'Even a fish can only drink so much of the sea'

Saying

ONE

Human freedom is in being who you were always meant to be. The seed of *Yourself* was always within you, otherwise you would not be here. There is a *You* within that body of yours. And it is connected to the 'YOU' that is beyond your body. Now, how are you going to grow the seed of the *you* within this material reality into which you have emerged?

Listen to the signs that you give yourself – that you have always given yourself. The signs are given through you throughout your life – now it is a moment to put them together. There is no genuine freedom until you arrive back to yourself, and be complete. There is a journey for you here. The myths have referred to this as the 'Hero's Journey' – as the 'Journey through the Underworld' – before arriving at the other side, a completed person. Yet where is this 'underworld'? Is it under the earth? No – it is here, the life of the Machine. It is the very material world: a world you need to move through in order to arrive at the point where you can move through the material world freely because you no longer resonate at its level. Now you roam freely.

Operation: Human Freedom is about finding your freedom whilst still in this material reality. You shall be walking upon the same Earth - yet your reality will be different. You shall be walking in the same physical body - yet your *being* will be different. It is You that you are bringing into Being.

We could not arrive at this point until we had first given you the messages in Volume 1 and Volume 2. Each of those volumes were stages in order to assist you to arrive here. The different parts of your being have to be shifted in order to be re-calibrated. In the past, this was undertaken by long processes, many of which were originally prescribed by religious or spiritual paths. There were many times when the 'initiation' involved being taken out of life, away from one's culture, in order to undergo the transformative process. One of the reasons for this was that an isolated society needed to accumulate and concentrate the necessary energy to impact the person's process. This is no longer the case. There are sufficient 'energetic impacts' now available within the world-at-large.

The seeker of human freedom – of transformation and liberty – need not locate themselves in a 'select community' that is secluded from society. The genuine freedom seeker can now live visible to the Machine's 'suspicion radar.' Now, you can walk amongst your society and culture, undetected, for the freedom to be obtained is within you. Your body is your vessel, and the sheath that conceals the secret, for *the secret protects itself.*

At this stage, it is the process of allowance that shall give greatest progress upon the path to internal freedom. Freedom comes through the human *becoming* shifting into the human *being*. To BE means that you are integrated with the rest of Intelligence. You are not a singular individual trapped within a flesh automaton. If you are afraid of losing your human personality, you are not yet prepared.

The personality is the *persona*. As we discussed in Volume One, the persona is a false construct. It is the 'you' that you believe you are. You are here, we suspect, because you have already moved beyond belief. Freedom must first be arrived at within yourself before any physical liberty will have meaning. In these coming times of physical constraint, the path to freedom is twofold. One, it is your own freedom to BE the genuine *essential self* that is the localized expression in this lifetime. Two, it is the freedom of humanity to exercise its freewill to be its own self-governing species on this planet. The individual is within humanity, and humanity is within the individual.

These messages are intended to assist the individual at the same time as focusing on the planetary level. There can be no separation between the one and the other. Without a healing upon the planetary level, individual evolvement will be made more difficult, as there will be continued enslavement and control of the human race. The universal laws, as already stated in this series, should also be applied at the greater planetary focus and not used solely for individual gain. If applied at the planetary level, this shall also benefit all individual life expressions as your reality exists as a holographic structure. By focusing upon the planetary whole, the individual also 'attracts' the flow of expansive energies into their own range of experience. The 'highest good of all' is when all elements and aspects are interrelated and understood as such.

Expansive and energetic forces are in re-calibration and re-arrangement mode at this time. There is constant motion, and the initial momentum has been gained. You are not pushing from a full-stop position but are participating in an already in-movement momentum. For this reason, chaotic energies are to be seen, felt, and experienced across your planetary life experiences. It is suggested that people do not get distraught or energetically entangled in these chaotic nodes, yet maintain focus and intention. Some of these processes need to be allowed to play out. Even without knowing or understanding the outcome, allowance of forces in play is necessary. Remember that allowance is also a form of release. And without release of certain energies there is no 'space' for the new, recalibrated energies to enter.

Existence has always been a cooperative participation. In past times, various forms of 'sacred rituals' were used to 'allow' the infusion of energies into the material sphere. People sensed that 'energies' were passing through and into operation, yet there was no education or knowledge-framework in which to comprehend these processes. Here, we are sharing with you some of these processes and their operation upon the planet and throughout your history in the forms of – like attraction, focused intention-manifestation, allowance, and balance and harmony. These incoming vibratory frequencies of energy require the cooperation of 'receiving minds' in which to find dispersal and transmission within your reality-matrix.

It is now possible to achieve more 'minds in agreeance' with this mergence and focus. Each individual component is a point of foci that contributes to the success of the overall plan for human evolvement upon this planet. The intended outcome is more important than the 'hows' and 'wherefores' – hence, many practices in your past were established with other reasons governing them in order to gather people together. People participated for the 'good of all' without knowing the essential core processes. Individual benefits were accrued for their contribution whilst the 'bigger plan' moved on.

The dog barks whilst the caravan moves on

Too much small-mind questioning can get in the way of the larger processes functioning. The long process of the Operation: Human Freedom upon this planet has had to take place 'in the shadows,' so to speak, without the majority of people having any knowledge or understanding. It was for their benefit, and humans have benefited in ways beyond description. Without this Operation, we can say that human life would not be where it is today. Now, to a greater extent than previously, we can make some public knowledge available of this Operation. That is why a certain 'allowance' is needed on the part of humanity, in giving commitment to their contribution to be utilized without getting themselves in the way of the process.

Whereas in the past, personification with a deity was used for people to identity with relational aspects of the Unity-Individual mergence of energies, this is no longer necessary. Identification with any 'external' entity is not a requirement – it is now a hindrance. There is no external-internal demarcation. There is only a vibratory scaling between resonance frequencies of Unified Intelligence. Remember, there **is no void within you**. You are filled. You can now drop the need to identify outside of yourself. It is time now to allow yourself to become a fractal part of the complete picture.

Human becoming is a becoming into wholeness. Separation is a perceptual illusion of the perception-control construct. Freedom is in unity.

TWO

It is time to be empowered. Power has become a corruptible force for it has become the tool of a physical hand of brutality and control. The original meaning and use of power has always been for constructive, developmental purposes. Power can be a *force* for good. Power is also an intangible potential, not only a material weapon. Time now to take back personal power, by bringing it back home to yourself. Power is also a belief in yourself. Power is a center of gravity that revolves within your very being. It is a combination of intent, self-belief, integrity, trust, and an unswerving knowing in doing the right thing. Power is not something to be wielded over others. Understand the nature of power by how people and institutions attempt to wield it over you – learn from this. Then make the distinction with how power flows through you.

Empowerment cannot come from an external source. There are external triggers that can activate a person into their own empowerment – yet it cannot be given as a 'thing' from outside of a person. External forms of power are not the same as empowerment. Remember, external forms of material power more often than not are working towards **disempowerment** of the individual and of humanity. True power and freedom are an inside job.

There are many elements available in the world as 'awakening tools' to personal power and freedom, leading to increased cognition and perception. It is also to be acknowledged, however, that there are far more 'mesmerizing tools' than awakening ones – the restraining forces have always outweighed the empowering ones in terms of quantity. They do not, importantly, outweigh in value and quality. Your material reality has become the reign of quantity that has sought to eclipse the power of essence. *Seek the essence and not the covering.*

The operation against human awakening is one that requires constant reinforcement. It is for this reason why it is persistent and pervasive – it needs to be in order to maintain its agenda. An observant glance over human history can reveal to the knowing eye the ever-constant apparatus of power and control that have been established and utilized to restrain the natural evolutionary lineage of the human species. Now that evolutionary impulse is seeking to come into manifestation for it has accumulated force through continued restraint. A dam of energy can only be held back for so long. The counter measure to this is that the controlling Machine has needed to acquire persistent upgrades to maintain its function. And at this time, it is seeking perhaps its most potent upgrade. For this reason, the current stakes are high indeed. Yet correct discernment from a place of inner knowing of the individual can cause all their layers of conditioning to crash. The activation of inner awareness has the power to burn away the tentacles of external entrapment almost instantly. Conscious awareness and awakening are a most powerful force for the individual.

A correct trigger - be it a phrase, message, or set of messages - can go directly into the body-mind of a person and literally 'rings true' with their entire nervous system. The result is a full bodily knowing. Once this bodily knowing occurs, it is sensed as a wave throughout the bodily system and conscious awareness. This then re-wires the functionality of the body-mind to receive upon a different resonance. This vibratory resonance process was dealt with in detail in Volume Two.

It is partly the function of those people operative within the Work to provide activation triggers for others. The method by which this is done is *all* methods.

The primary intention for the individual seeking perceptual freedom is the need to change the current life experience upon the planet. The existing paradigm of human experience needs to be seen and perceived clearly for the corruption that it is. Those who can see and accept this have the capacity for further development and empowerment. Otherwise, these messages would not have appealed to you. You were drawn to them for you were awaiting them. All things come to those who wait. Once the individual perception begins to shift through a new receptivity of consciousness, many elements in life - including sayings, tales, expressions, etc. - will now be recognized for the consciousness triggers that they are. You will then come to the realization that your life experience has been surrounded with material - tools - for your awakening. It is only that, as we stated previously - *you cannot see what you cannot see.* Yet now, the more you notice these 'planted seeds' the more your conscious perception will be triggered. Once this process is begun, it remains active and is irreversible. It is as if an accumulative momentum. As if within a good story, one 'clue' may lead to another, as a series of 'synchronicities' enter your life experience – as if on cue.

Be alert to comments, news stories, a media program, and so on, for aspects will start to fit into a new context for you – start to recognize your triggers. The more you do so, the more you shall be activating your own dormant abilities. Your contexts of meaning will change for you now. This is likely to also affect particular friendships – some new contacts will increase in importance in your life whilst some present ones will diminish. This is an outward sign of your inward reshuffling and recalibration. Your thoughts and focus will also find a new direction and context. Your life will align more greatly with the Work. Your life will become the Work – you will sense this deeply. You will find yourself naturally aligning to a new direction of your attention and focus, with a renewed concentration of energy. The intent shall now become directed towards the attainment of that which is for the greater good of humanity. Your future accomplishments will be tied to the strength of your focus from this moment forward.

Humanity is no longer tied only to the hemispheres of their minds – humanity is now connected across global hemispheres. Physical connections are the external replications of internal relations. The internal structure was always present - dormant for most people - until outer connectivity reflects to them their innate state of human self. The focal point begins with the individual yet goes broadly beyond this localized point. The human being is a focal point in space and time for broader spectrum influences - both across terrestrial and dimensional zones. For the future transcendence of humanity upon its evolutionary path, a global consciousness is required. The individual lights need to start coming on so that the whole house will eventually wake up.

Previously, localized foci of conscious awakening was easier to target, control, and/or eliminate - processes of change could be blocked from further development. Pockets of development could be contained. Now you are no longer in the 'pocket phase' - it has become widespread. Operation: Human Freedom has entered the next stage of manifestation. This involves allowance and mergence - themes that shall apply to these messages.

THREE

Any desired outcome requires great self-discipline to retain the focus, commitment, and concentrated effort. The outcome of the 'bigger picture' is not visible – and may indeed be constantly shifting – according to revisions and influences along its course. The urge to be involved in this Work is a *force of being* – it cannot be sustained by superficial or externally-driven desires. It can only be sustained from an internal knowing, and a commitment that needs no outer confirmation.

There will be surprise or serendipitous events along the way that shall renew and refresh one's energy. Remember, the individual is participating in an energetic dynamic – there are bound to be energized impulses made available along the Way. As more localized aspects of awakening occurs across your societies, these shall be adding to an already present, and moving, dynamic. It is, to use a known analogy, like adding more snow to a rolling snowball. The momentum accelerates in force and inevitability. This growing force becomes increasingly felt within the collective consciousness of humanity, allowing further triggering.

The external power forces of the Machine and its controllers do not largely focus on the individual consciousness. They observe, track, and analyze the collective mass consciousness, and steer their efforts onto this. For this reason, the Operation of the Work has been to awaken the consciousness of the individual - one at a time if need be. Every time an individual consciousness gains heightened perception, this adds exponentially to the collective - not singularly. As we have stated, the 'flip-turn' will come when not expected for it does not require nor follow a linear trajectory. The lack of focus from the controlling forces on the individual shifting allows an unrecognized momentum to gain traction. If enough momentum can be gained, then this will dissolve the overall reach of the general mind programming that the Machine implements across humanity. Certain critical or 'crisis points' will be moved through along the way. If enough of these are surpassed, then more energy from external sources is likely to be made available for humanity. Keep in mind that there is a significant, and important, difference between calling for assistance, and calling **to be of** assistance.

Do not wait around for interventions from outside. The interventions shall be coming from each of you as you awaken, perceive, and *intervene* to influence the current perception-reality that constrains humanity. Humankind has to work out its own solution to the dilemma it is in. You can be helped to help yourself, but don't expect any big sky ships to arrive any time soon with supplies! Your destiny has to be your own story. If you do not create your own story, then humanity has no true legacy. To pass off your own story by taking another's is a form of plagiarism. There can be no plagiarism in the cosmic narrative. You are now being compelled to write your own script – surprise yourselves. Choose your strength for you have it. It has always been yours to acknowledge and own. There is power in receiving ownership. This can also be done in owning, first of all, the small decisions and choices you make, as you move to take back your own power of Selfhood. Each step in your day-to-day lives is a step that becomes a part of who you are or wish to be. Do not neglect the smaller steps for they make the whole. Every step gains energy to which it contributes to the larger life experience.

These new emerging patterns of energy are necessary to replace the breakdown of the old patterned order. This older order of patterned energy across the planet is no longer in cohesion. It has been breaking down for some time – for many of your centuries. This dis-coherence of the whole patterning is coming to a noticeable end point in your physical manifestation. There is no longer any possibility of it being ignored by less aware people upon the planet. The focus of individuals is not to 'jump' into 'repair mode' because they do not understand the major forces that are involved across the planet. Your focus is for individual awakening to a new perceptive-driven expression of life experience. And in this focus, to become triggers for others also. Work with and amongst the people.

Smaller increments of change at the ground-level can cause major influence upon larger systems. The power of change available at this ground-level is remarkable. All the more reason for the Machine to keep it well under guard and control. Yet once the 'Genie' is out of the box – as they say – then there is no going back. This Genie has freewill. Consider this – freewill thought roaming as a creative force through your reality-structure. Creative 'thought-thinking' that acts as a conduit for incredible manifesting energies within a limitless creative cosmos. There is currently a lack of creative freewill and expression within your planetary life expression. It has been silenced within you. The masses shout and gasp but do not engage in its magnificence. The human splendor has been silenced under a sheath of ignorance. Time now for purposeful intent for human freedom and the expression of creative freewill.

There shall be no lack of challenges for you in these times. This is, and will continue to be, abundantly clear. Many opportunities will present themselves in varying aspects, and can be utilized to gain understanding in different realms of the life experience. For those that participate in challenging events, the benefits are likely to be considerable. It is about keeping one's head amidst challenging, and often chaotic, environments. The advantages of a clear and calm state of mind and being will become very clear to you. The peace and stability acquired when within the 'eye of the storm' is priceless. Also, giving more trust to the inner instinct that provides a 'bodily knowing' in the instant. People tend to habitually go to the mind for an analysis of the situation, and to place an 'intellectual framework' upon what is perceived.

In this instance, bodily knowing is blocked out and the *knowing sense* is dulled, often to detrimental value. The more trust that is given to the knowing sense, the more it actively engages within the life experience. It is You - a part of you that is usually overlooked and ignored. There are many parts of you now that need to be brought together, into coherent correspondence. The practice of this *inner listening* will help to break patterned habits. It is the habitual patterns that are relied upon by the controllers of your social programming. This they have analyzed to the tenth degree, and they feel comfortable in knowing you. Your controllers are complacent in believing they know humanity inside and out. They believe there is not much else left within you, and that you do not have any surprise for them. This is reason enough, is it not, to create that surprise?

Feel into what is the most appropriate response. Do not react in automatic, known patterns. It is time to reprogram the general conscious awareness that you have been carrying around with you. As we have stated before - do not be playing **their game**. In each moment, be aware and conscious of your awareness. Be present with yourself in your everyday moments.

Be mindful of those feelings that denote tension, anxiety, or worry – take them into observation early and clearly. Pay attention to that which irks you, and find its source calmly. Find your own solutions before your habits intervene to provide their cure. Ask yourself first always, before you consider approaching another. The more trust and belief that is given to the Self, the more the self becomes validated and feels its active presence is of worth. Confidence in your own beginning to reach your own ends is paramount.

Consider that there are many more others like yourself, even if you may not know of them or be aware of them in your physical life. By accepting this commitment, you are aligning yourself with others of your ilk. Your contribution is in accordance with responsibility. The more commitment and contribution that is given from you – whether materially or energy-intention – the more responsibility becomes you. Do not think of this in terms of 'reward' – or even 'punishments' – for these are the carrots and the sticks that your Machine has programmed into your thinking patterns. Genuine relations work upon reciprocal energies in due and correct proportion.

Appropriate participation requires appropriate words and actions in their right moments. An individual in this Work of Operation: Human Freedom is responsible for their deliverance and appropriate use of words and actions. Playing the fool can be fun – but don't play the fool with your Self.

True consciousness change requires dedicated intent and purpose to shift the focus of the human life experience. The intent to change consciousness should be the more focused intent than others. Each single triggering of a localized aspect of consciousness can go unnoticed; yet the spread of consciousness change within the collective is noticeable. The origin of the spread cannot be targeted for it shall not be found. The rising wave shall ripple out as if from unknown beginnings. Individual shift contributes to the evolvement of that individual as well as contributing to the planetary shift as a whole – awakening is not a singular purpose or gain. The true rebellion is the one that rises not within the visible spotlight.

As the resonance of the collective consciousness shifts, this will contribute to dissolve the constraints that have held back the human mindset into restricted patterns. Human freedom is a release from these imperceptible patterns that hold a mind within its prison. Do not wait around for external assistance to arrive when you are the assistance you have been waiting for.

FOUR

Freedom requires the discernment to recognize genuine information and truths from within the increased broadcast of lies and mixed half-truths. The gameboard is becoming increasingly messy, deliberately so. The controlling powers are intent on confusing human minds, and of pushing them back into uncertainty and then slumber as each begins to awaken slightly. That is why individual awakening must be a silent affair – in humility and without announcement. Do not announce your arrival before you have arrived. To do so would make sure your arrival will be greeted!

The tool for true discernment is within all yet latent within most. Time to polish this instrument and use it regularly on all input and incoming information. More mist is coming into the wayfarer's path; more poison into the waters. The ability to discern is now critical in allowing experience to be filtered into wisdom. Without correct discernment, invasive elements, such as memes and trigger-slogans, enter into the mind alongside planted doubts and confusions. When there is no sure understanding, hesitancy creeps in. Hesitancy soon grows into self-doubt. Once a person has self-doubt, a corrosive intrusion has occurred. A balanced and trusting discernment is a self-tool that can replace the need for judgement. Judgement can be swayed into criticizing others and self. It is a pattern of mind that the Machine uses to create division among people and uncertainty and doubt within them. Judgement is a programmed faculty that uses pre-planted opinions and beliefs for its functioning. It is therefore an external tool that people use as a two-edged sword. Contrary to this, discernment is a faculty that can be activated within each person. It can be uniquely theirs and is attuned to their unique self. Polish this instrument in order to replace judgement. In the times ahead, judgement potentials will be further corrupted as external programming and propaganda targets and deliberately damages the ability to judge appropriately.

With discernment comes insight. Take this word – 'in' and 'sight.' It signifies inner vision – the capacity of interior perception. This is true discernment. This inner vision is able to perceive the essence of a thing, beyond the projection. The Machine is a master of projections and manipulations. There are further, more elaborate and complex projections planned in these upcoming times. Many people around you will be falling immediately into the trap of 'believing the hype' and of taking sides. This again will be a sign of the limited potentials of personal judgement. Do not judge friends for their actions. Discern that they may be acting from ignorance and from targeted propaganda. Discernment can help you avoid falling into the reactive mode. It also allows a degree of necessary detachment. Do you see how judgement utilizes emotional patterns whereas discernment does not? Be aware of those 'behavioral positions' you take that have pre-programmed mental and emotional states within them. We caution you not to act from 'behavioral sets' but to respond from your unique center of self and detachment.

Some things are always given up in the path to freedom. This creates necessary space in creating a shift. *Take with you that which you would save from a sinking ship.* Would you run to grab the luggage, or would you save yourself? When you make this perceptive shift within you, all circumstances are shown within a new context. Then you can operate within those new contexts. Through a release of the old, new solutions are made more visible. The path to wisdom from within oneself is made more accessible. The path to freedom is first an inward one, to access what has always been available to you. One must make a step within in order to take the following steps forward. This access to personal experience can help lift a person out of the everyday morass of judgment, opinions, and reckless thought patterns. It is time to shift your view of life.

Freedom for the self is not to be found through the talk, opinions, chatter – the constant flow of noise – that fills the external environment. You cannot talk your way into freedom. To find your way out, you must first step within. To engage in your personal freedom, you must first disengage from the external attractors of the human life. Not to disengage in terms of physically finding a refuge; rather, to detach through shifting energetic resonance. This was discussed in Volume 2. Your keys will be found now through the internal conversation. Those external, daily conversations from which people 'know' you will be affected. By changing your internal patterns of conversation, your external 'social conversational' patterns will also shift. Do not be concerned if those around you no longer find you 'entertaining.' They will say that you no longer engage with them in the same way. Note how true this is - you will not be *engaging* with these exterior patterns in the same way. You too will notice your new shift into greater detachment. What you are engaged in now is shifting your life patterns through an internal re-wiring. From this, there will be a shifting in your exterior life patterns, as you have recalibrated the inner resonation. This will operate through a new position of discernment. The world does not just 'happen' to people – it is affected from the place you allow yourself to come from. Many causes in life come from the life experience patterns that people project. Each person projects an energetic pattern from which life experience responds. Change your energetic patterning - a different life experience will respond. This is your responsibility of choice.

Have you yet taken full responsibility for your energetic patterns? How do you consider your life as a reflection of your internal state? These two positions should begin to create a relative match. If they do not, then more interior work is necessary in order to align with a corresponding exterior life experience. If there is any imbalance, then the source is always an interior one first. Denial of personal responsibility is a dominant form of blockage for many people. A person needs to be discerning of their own patterns – of energetic habits and forms – and to recognize that which is attuned to their intended life experience and which are now part of the older patterning and in need of release. There is no necessity to be locked into a patterned life experience that is not wished for. Do not lock yourself into an unwanted pattern experience. If you wish to change, you must create the genuine desire to do so – then make this desire into a necessity. This may take time, and constant small corrections, until the desired pattern of life experience is reached. If intent and purpose are held in focus and concentration, the patterns must change. It is your responsibility to stay the course.

The things spoken of here may sound 'simple' and may be regarded as not important for the path of personal evolvement. We indicate this is not so. That which appears simple may only be so from a patterned perspective. Each person needs to develop their power of discernment that is genuine and truthful. A discerning eye upon one's own aspects is crucial. Consider your attitudes, opinions, thoughts, and statements. It takes a genuine and uncorrupted eye of discernment to objectively perceive the truth of one's own attitudes and thoughts – does it not? It is expected that each person, in some form, attempts to fool themselves.

This is a pattern within a controlled human nature. Part of the larger control is that a person is subtly conditioned to attempt, throughout their lives, to fool themselves. An ongoing battle-with-self takes up so much personal resources that there is often no energy remaining for focused intent on true liberation.

You will be called upon to discern from that information which is untrue. The sharper this internal discernment faculty, the clearer your focus of perception. You are no longer in a position to be taking in all information and external impacts without filter. To move toward the greater Reality, the individual's filtering mechanism must be sharp and accurate. Do not allow all that rushes at you to enter within you. Be stronger to block out the unwarranted. Brush it away from you – energetically declare that you do not accept or wish this external influence to enter. Take charge of your own Gateway. Become your own guard of discernment. It is time now to actively protect your inner world from unwanted external influences.

Actively state, spoken within your mind, that you will practice discernment before you begin to listen, watch, or engage with external information. State your intention before you are exposed to the impact. You will not give your permission for unruly or untruthful impacts to enter your inner domain. Why should you? In this way, the 'knowing' intelligence that resides within your body-mind complex will become activated to discern and filter all incoming information, and often will make instinctive decisions on your conscious and unconscious behalf. Each individual pattern of experience has a different ability to establish this faculty of discernment. And like any muscle, it can also be strengthened by correct use.

What is your faculty of discernment indicating to you now, as you read these messages? Learn to remember the flavor of genuine truth recognition.

FIVE

The sequence of disruptive events in your outer world will seem to grow in proportion to the sensed acceleration of passing linear time. In this complex mixture, each individual must 'make' their own sense. This is hard to accomplish if you are caught within the cloak of captive persuasion. There are also chaotic events within different geographical zones that are each spiraling into increased disruption. So many human beings are now caught within an energetic circle of disruptive influence. It is critical that those people seeking personal freedom from the perceptual prison create circumstances that give them safety from unruly influences. The energy pattern of inflicted trauma will increase and spread. This is an energetic pattern to avoid. By creating deliberate detachment from these traumatic patterns, such individuals can assist in forming energetic patterns of equilibrium to counteract these forces. This form of balancing is very necessary in these times.

There are plans from the controlling forces to increase chaotic events to the point where balancing energies are no longer functional or viable. There are forces of what may be termed as 'negative vibrations' constantly acting against the resonance of positive-polarity vibrations. There is a long-term plan in progress that wishes to create a permanent 'negative resonance' for the planet and for humanity. A permanent resonance of this type of vibration would then dominate and block interventions from the positive resonance. This is part of the Game that is being played out. To achieve this, the minority controllers have attempted over time to lower the vibrational fields of the human inhabitants so that they become 'attuned' to a planet of lower vibration. This has been sought through various technological methods and installations, as well as through environmental and 'health' related domains. This is an ambitious Game to shift the entire polarity of this planet and to affect the complete life experience of humanity. There is also a great degree of instability within this plan. The question, more than ever, is the integrity of human freewill. Human freewill is at the core of the human path to freedom.

Greater evolvement requires greater degrees

of responsibility. Just as an adult in your world takes on more responsibility as they mature in life experience - so is it the same with maturity of evolvement. The main focus from the Machine has been to make people undesirable to change. If change is not desired, then the status quo can be extended - and amplified. To desire change is a question of human freewill. The genuine desire for freedom must come from within the individual and collective consciousness of humankind. This is the focal point. And this is the inevitable target for the apparatus, methods, and institutions of control. At the same time, there are 'positive thought interventions' surrounding the various layers of the planet awaiting for individual and collective freewill access and the allowance for people's thinking to be activated into recognizing the need for change.

The need for change has to become activated in many more individuals. These will then spread their energy to catalyze others into awakening into change. Each person who begins to awaken to the situation can play a part. Not everyone who begins to perceive the nature of their deception will desire to focus on full evolvement. The path of individual and collective evolvement is a complex and committed one. Yet there are other roles to perform in the path toward freedom for the human species. Some of those individuals triggered into greater awareness will choose to rebel against the system of the Machine. This shall at least create visual awareness of the situation. It is not the path of deep transformation, yet it too can be utilized as a distraction method. Such physical protest is not a true path, and only suggested for temporary methods of distraction by certain individuals. Whilst there are those people creating physical and visible protest to the systems, others are operating at deeper depths - quite literally - below the radar of the controllers.

Be aware that whatever you resist, you are sustaining. By resisting the systems of the Machine, you are acknowledging the structure of the control system. This reinforces its existence in your reality. By protesting the system, you are recognizing it. When you recognize a thing, you project a validity to it in your constructed reality. See the Game that is being played now? The controllers are very aware of this. Not only do they expect this reaction - they purposefully orchestrate it into being. By doing so, they play the people like puppets into pre-ordained positions and expected movements. It is a gameplay awaiting for your unconscious arrival. Those who are conscious arrive elsewhere.

There is a noticeable conscious receptivity to this situation now – and to messages such as these. There is an energetic triggering occurring within many individuals. Some are sensing this urge to see 'beyond the veil,' as if on time. These are the 'choice points' we spoke of earlier. Many such decision moments are arriving now for people. Even within this reality of polarity that dominates your domain, there is a clear distinction of choice between choosing *Life* and choosing *anti-life*. This may sound dramatic to you. Within the bigger picture, this is closer to an actuality. Within the larger scale, these coming decisions are indeed of vast significance for the future of humanity. And it all begins with you making the right smaller decisions and acting on those choices within your daily life experiences. There is a vast 'bigger picture' of which you do not currently need to concern yourselves with. Accomplish the immediate need that is in front of you first. Move forward by making the necessary incremental steps. Allow, in trust, that these shall all correspond to the shifts within the larger picture. Everything is interconnected – be assured in this. There are no separate parts within the whole Reality. The fragmentation exists only within your perceptual prison and within the construct of the Machine.

The intention for human freedom becomes its own attractor. There are correspondences with other frequencies of energy that align with the freedom intention. This intention must exist alongside the focus for human becoming. There is no distinction. Genuine human becoming can only exist within the energetic space of freedom. To not have this trajectory of freedom blocks the evolution of the human species, and the fullness of human becoming. If you wish to commit to a future, then commit to the future of being fully human.

To repeat, the focus and intention for human freedom cannot succeed if it clings to older patterns. If humanity resorts to older patterns of retaliation and revenge, then the new patterning will not uphold. There will be no resonance of vibratory alignment. Is this clear? There is a need to drop all older programming patterns in order to engage on the path of genuine human freedom. This is a freedom for you to choose freewill in how you live – not to access the old programming over and over again. Your focus must not be turned upon that which you are leaving behind. There is no going forward when the eye is on the rearview mirror.

The choice point for the trajectory ahead is an opportunity to choose a genuine human future over a heavily controlled and managed life experience that blocks the evolvement to become fully human. The controllers, and those that operate within the Machine, have striven to inculcate repeated patterns within the human life experience. Your history has become a narrative of repeated programs. Many of these are deliberately re-released - they re-surface - for programs of cultural repetition. These repetitions are devices to further instill the pattern into the channels of human conditioning. Repetition enforces programming. Look at your cycles of history - do you not recognize repeated patterns? Look at your patterns of orchestrated civil protest. Have these repeated patterns succeeded or largely failed in their objectives? The picture begins to fall into place when seen from this perspective of distance and perception of greater clarity.

Your planet now requires enough individuals who have evolved beyond the conditioning of repeated patterning. Such repetitions of the life experience must be recognized and transcended in order to align with bringing into your planetary reality a new paradigm of the life experience. This is the task that lies ahead for the human species. This is the task of Operation: Human Freedom.

SIX

The individual life experience in your reality is aligned with the good of the planetary whole. Your experiences within your manifestation upon this planet are aligned with corresponding to the future of the planet. You are not apart from it, but exist as a part of the planetary experience. The collective traumatization of the human species through the perception prison of control has also affected the balance and harmonic systems of your planet. This is now noticeable to you. It is time to take responsibility for the relations between that of your individual consciousness with the planetary consciousness. There are fields within fields, and none are within a vacuum. Only your deception has created this ignorance and has fostered your ideas of separation. There is no separation at the fundamental level. This splintering in your perception plays into your own incarceration and stigmatizes your understanding. When you are splintered, so is your understanding and store of knowledge.

> When you are still fragmented,
> lacking certainty –
> what difference does it make
> what your decisions are?
>
> Hakim Sanai (1050-1131)

It is sometimes the case that people who believe themselves to be whole are in fact fragmented. Further, those people not consciously aware of their state can also be in greater resonance with the whole. Many of these less consciously aware individuals - yet more aligned with the whole - are contributing to the overall planetary consciousness without their awareness. There are many roles that people can take. Yet focused concentration provides the greatest resource for it is aligned with intention. Intention with focus creates a more dynamic manifestation, as we explained previously.

The accomplishments you bring to your life experience need not apply to your social notions of achievement. You have created around you a system of status and fame that is captivating for so many. Your cultural perceptions are programmed by these artificial measurements. Fame is praised as a great achievement by many in your societies. These people are then worshipped and often brought further into the social control construct of the Machine. Fame is not a path of liberation, although it may bring you many fruits. In our view, the measurement of fame ties a person down into greater layers of the program. The program gives you the measurement that many do abide and judge by. Contributions to the aim of human freedom from perceptive imprisonment are more limited from the pedestal of social admiration. There are many contributions of great worth gifted by those who lead lives not recognized by the masses. These are the silent operators. They often operate in simplicity - and with greater ease. You never know whom you may meet!

There are also those individuals who bring great focus onto the manifestation of negativity. Are these people providing a function - of course they are. It is also necessary at this time to have those individuals and groups who bring the negative into focus for the mass consciousness to acknowledge its presence. It is the same with any disease of the body. The disease is brought into view so that the ailment can be recognized, and action taken. It is often the case that you cannot heal what you do not know ails you. There are those people also who bring negativity to the surface in order for healing and recalibration to be applied. These people may not be consciously aware of what their role is in this way; yet this function assists the positive path to realization and freedom. It can be said then that there are times when there are no clear players. That is why we put forth the notion of discernment, and the necessity to refrain from quick judgement without correct perception. There are layers within layers in the Game. We can state here too that there are individuals, now as in history, who draw negative forces to them. Their cause becomes one of increased negativity. But this is to draw all energies to a crisis point so that a critical juncture and/or shift may occur. Some transformations take operative energies from opposing forces in order to fuel their cause. Does this make sense to you?

Some purposes within the life experience are to draw particular energies into attraction. Without a perception of the bigger picture, it cannot be known what the outcome of these actions are. Within the polarity reality of your domain it appears that there are two sides – the truth is that all sides are in some way interrelated in that there are no separations, only energetic alignments. It is for this reason that we suggest not to fall into the 'polarity game' of making judgements upon others according to what is observed externally. Each individual is to find what is important for them within the moment - to accomplish those aims that are felt to be of significance by listening to the interior guide. Following the inner guidance will not only be of greater necessity but also of greater difficulty as the outer environment becomes increasingly coercive. Feel and sense what is appropriate for you, and do not be concerned what may be appropriate for others - each person must come to their own understanding on what is fitting to them. At this stage, the individual must follow their way to reach their goals. The contribution to the collective will be better aligned when it comes from a more realized and aware individual - from a person who has 'arrived' through their own steps. Work on yourself in order to then be of greater benefit to others. By allowing yourself to become, you then allow others to become.

Many a person has begun their path to personal freedom and awareness only to have this goal 'influenced out' of them through social pressures, distractions, and other external impacts. Remembrance to one's own aim is of importance here. Be compelled to remain 'on track' with your intentions. This may then attract certain 'synchronicities' into your life which are good signals for the life experience.

There are other humans who understand the imperative for human freedom from the present system of bondage. They also understand that the controlling powers on this planet have withheld much crucial information from the populace. Since this is the case, it also suggests that most, if not all, current and historical social and cultural institutions cannot be trusted. It has been such institutions – including state and religious bodies – that have deliberately withheld important knowledge from the people. There is now much knowledge and information circulating through your communication channels. Your present channels of access to information is a support for you to accomplish your own research and gain individual understanding. Use them whilst they remain relatively 'open.' There are plans to lock down these communication channels into further control. Such resources in that domain are time-limited.

Individual and collective knowledge and awareness is a critical component in calling forth humanity's freedom from oppression. There is no blame game here. Humanity also needs to take responsibility for allowing itself to be duped and deluded by the system. There have been, and continue to be, those who are waiting for humanity to awaken. To awake and come into awareness - and then to declare their collective intention to break from this deception. Humanity - individually and collectively - needs to make this declaration. Then other assistance aligned with universal laws can come into play.

Make the declaration - awake into a new activity of experience.

SEVEN

Each person can receive the call to awaken into assistance - yet only the few will respond. Those that do respond can also be of assistance to others. We repeat - by helping yourself you are then helping others. The few who awaken are important here. They are like the beacons - the burning bright lights that help to guide others in their moments of darkness. This does not need to sound dramatic, for it is a rendering of the truth. A few awakened individuals can assist thousands more - yet thousands of non-awakened sleeping people can assist none. The individual should first take care of their own awakening before thinking of others. As it is said:

"Do not think that your magic ring will work if you are not yourself Solomon"'

Regardless of your awareness, you are bound to the physical planet and to the populace of this planet. The fate of the populace will be your fate also. You knew this before, and you are again to be reminded of this. There is much at stake. Whilst those individuals of awareness can be better prepared, and also protected, during these times, they remain as participants upon this planet. What goes off here, goes off for all. Yet the destiny of the individual is not the destiny of the many - and in this you create your own. The destiny of a person of knowledge is different.

Not only does the individual have the right to know about themselves and the situation, they also have a right to know what is blocking them from knowing of these things. Only when a human being is truly free will they come to learn of their destiny, and their origin. These opportunities exist for each, yet they must be 'found' and recognized. Feel yourself into these messages and whether they speak of a truth for you. You can then decide and take your own response from this. The path of freedom to evolve may not be for everyone. There are many differing ways to participate in the overall plan. For many reading these messages, the compulsion to engage in the evolvement process toward human freedom will be strong. It is what has brought you here. Those individuals who are aware and who resonate with this information, they are asked to focus their intent and accelerate their awareness. The time is now. Work should have begun yesterday.

Plans within plans are rapidly unfolding across this planet. Events have been in preparation for this moment for a long period of planning. What you are currently experiencing are not 'accidental' events or unexpected anomalies. Matters have been very carefully controlled and orchestrated - and continue to be so. It is incredible to perceive the extent of the controller's planning. It is complex indeed. Yet outcomes remain variable, on all sides, according to how aspects emerge during these volatile times. Being volatile also means being vulnerable to the slightest inflections and influences. A slight nudge can cause a whole edifice to come apart. These are the times when interventions of awareness are most necessary and most effective.

The cycles of repetition must be broken. If not, then the same patterns shall be repeated, and this current civilization will fall the same way as past ones. Where are they now? Another inflection point has been reached - another crossroads of opportunity. It is hoped that this current phase of human civilization can make the transition into the next paradigm of life experience beneficial to evolvement. Time to make more positive use of human freewill. Within a reality of manifestation, the power of freewill to intend and focus is tremendous indeed. Intention is a tool that can manifest freedom for humanity if focused correctly, and if not aligned to manifesting only desires and the greed for continued distraction. The intent needs to be focused on creating a new paradigm of life experience on this planet. In order to achieve this, a break in the dysfunctional old systems, beliefs, and binding forces and programs needs to happen.

Ignorance of the situation can easily lead to arrogance. Arrogance can lead to complacency that then becomes a form of passiveness, which eventually becomes laziness. Ignorance is then a great vulnerability that many cannot see or be aware of. It is important that those who can, participate to assist in lessening this ignorance. Existence in these lower vibrational realms is not easy. Effort is required in order to participate in the energies of awakening and the activation of finer faculties of perception. There needs to be a push to meet the incoming energies that can assist the individual. What is within your destiny will not reach you if you remain seated, not making the required efforts. Whatever is there in potential for you needs to be met. Participation can begin from strengthening focused thought and intention. These are forms of energetic vibrations that create a 'welcoming' resonance for alignment.

The material form of the life experience is 'brought into being' by a focused thought intention. It is these energetic sources which hold everything 'in form.' The outward structure is only a reflection of the participating thought forms that give it existence. Think of an organization - it only exists so long as the people that make it up continue to give their thought and intention to the organization. If all these people left, then the organization would cease to operate - it would be lifeless. The basis of manifestation are the thought forms and intentions that participate in its material existence. Change these thought forms and you change the manifestation. Does this not sound appropriate? This is why so much planning and control has gone into the programming of human minds. To control what human minds process, and how they operate, gains control over the external manifestation. Operation: Human Freedom is about transforming how humans manifest their thoughts and intentions, and where they place their focus. In other words - how they think.

Freedom begins from thinking in the right way. That is, thought free from external corruptions. A preferred and desired outcome must be understood. Correct intentions must be held firmly in place.

A different path of adventures is possible - and awaits.

EIGHT

Each individual will be faced with the decision as to whether it is their role to participate in the transformation of humanity on this planet, or not. This decision can be made by no other. Once a decision has been made, then a commitment has simultaneously been taken. The next step would be to align with the resonance of that commitment. Those that do so may well find that a space within them begins to feel more filled. Purpose can bring great nourishment to a human being. Until a person can find and align with their dominant purpose, a sense of unfulfillment is often felt. Purpose strengthens one's essential identity – rather than the conditioned social persona. Have you recognized that many people, yourself included, often find it necessary to go 'searching' for something? This often entails varied changes in location, work positions, relationships, and even belief structures. The more compelling the search, the more the need to find one's identity of purpose.

When found, purpose can give great strength to the individual's intent and focus of manifestation. Human freedom has been curtailed and obstructed for so long through the endless supply of distractions. Further inventions and devices are planned to increase this field of distortion. If you give up the search for purpose, you slump back into the sea of distortion. Distortion works to block the quiet focus point from finding its harmony of resonance. It is as if there is static in the device, and the signal is not clear. Aligning with a focus of resonance (see Volume Two) will help to clear the static. Humanity has been unfairly blocked from its connection to the focused resonance of Source. This is, in modern parlance, a struggle between the Signal and the Noise.

The Noise keeps human brain activity and the nervous system in a state of 'artificial excitability.' This exacerbated state of activity negates the necessary coherence of the body-mind resonance. It is necessary for the awakening individual to seek out and find their resting point of awareness. The over-stimulation that is deliberately provided by the Machine creates dissonance within your thought processes. It is difficult to literally 'think straight.' There is a lack in a deep consideration of incoming thoughts. They are processed, as if a part of the factory conveyor line. Seldom are incoming thought messages reflected upon to the required degree. The consciousness field is superficially processed and filtered by the regular human body-mind complex – infrequently is it comprehended as intended. This is what we refer to as the 'dumbing down' of humanity.

People have been programmed and conditioned into running around. It is as if they are afraid of boredom. For the awakened person that perceives clearly, there is no such state as boredom. This too is a manufactured state – and many buy into its programming. Modes of relaxation become variations of Noise. From music to television to physical activities of stimulation. Fabricated forms of dissonance have been created to become surrogates for the original forms of relaxation. Stimulation is the name of the Game. Quiet time in modern societies has been invaded. It is time to unlearn the learned busyness of the Machine. The control system is now upgrading to keep you all wired-up to stimulation 24/7. Some people only slow down when they are forced to – by disease.

What is being brought to your consideration here is your focus of priorities. Those that wish to participate in aligning with a new expression of life experience on this planet must consider their priorities and, if necessary, realign. There can be no new resonance of manifestation if those engaged with the new paradigm are attached to the energies of old expressions. At the least, a reshuffling of priorities to give dominance to that which is correctly aligned to going forward. The new awareness will require a certain frequency of 'quiet space' in order to focus with intent. This will also entail a stepping back from the participation in meaningless pursuits. It is your freewill choice. As we said, with choice to commit comes responsibility.

Peace and calm are not easy to acquire in a modern environment when surrounded by urban impacts, noises, ongoing activity. Now that your airwaves are filled with unseen and contaminating vibrations and frequencies there is increased dissonance. Even if you do not see or perceive it, does not detract from its impact. There is deliberate reason why your global organizations are trying to encourage and persuade more of you to become urban dwellers. They are attempting to get as many as possible out of the rural areas and into crowded, urban spaces. These 'metropolises' are growing rapidly across the planet. Larger cities are becoming larger. There is only one alternative to manage this level of complexity – greater technological social control. Control in urban settings is much more manageable. In the megacity, the natural can be replaced by the artificial. The night sky is always highly polluted, from both within the earth orbit as well as on the ground. Light pollution will further deny humans the right to observe an evening sky.

Mobility, transport, and movement are all now 24/7 requiring your nights to be almost as lit and noisy as your days. Constant activity is becoming the consensus state of human civilization. Technology will further seal the permanence of this state. Do you not recognize the deliberate plan that is set up here? All this over-stimulation, activity, and life dissonance is further severing humanity's connection not only to the planet – the Earth resonance – but also with Source Field. Humanity is being gradually cut-off from the natural fields that sustain it. The natural order is being shifted into an artificial grid. This is the Machine that we spoke of previously. This precipitates a one-way flow of energies that takes away from the sustenance of your natural surroundings. It is critical that the human being returns to being of a reciprocal nature.

The individual can enhance the power of their presence in order to realign and reciprocate the energetic flows. The physical location of such aware and committed individuals is now a part of their path ahead. There will be some movement among those participating individuals. You may feel compelled now to make changes in your physical location. We suggest you listen carefully to your inner guides and consider the 'nudges' you sense within you. Be attentive to the choices and decisions that arrive in these times. Be clear in your intention to cultivate 'spaces of calm' within your everyday lives. It is important to be grounded now. The grounding can help in having a 'quieting effect' upon your life. Consider carefully your participation in any frantic or over-stimulating activity. We speak more in terms of energetic impacts than those of physical exercise.

Appreciate the self that you are. Be blessed in what you have and not be focused on the lack. Your intention here will shift the manifestation of your life experience - more than you know. It is important to seek and focus on the positive attributes in these disruptive times. Appreciate what you have now in order to attract the better attributes of what is to come. All energies of attention are related, regardless of time zones. A grateful heart will attract and resonate with those things and experiences that are likely to make you feel grateful for in the future. See the relation?

Make the relation happen.

NINE

The more you consider the new life expression to manifest on this planet, the more this becomes a real possibility. The collective concentration of the human species to focus intent on the new paradigm for the human becoming has great power to bring into manifestation. If it is not first real within *your* minds, then it shall not be made real for you. Keeping the concept of the human becoming within your mental attention is a first step in creating your liberty as a species. The more you focus on this idea, the more you create its potential. This is the 'behind the scenes' work that must be done in order to prepare the front-of-house show. You cannot pull a rabbit out of the hat if you first do not intend that there is a rabbit to manifest. Does this make sense?

Operation: Human Freedom will come about as a desired intent from those of humanity who wish to manifest a different life experience other than a form of slavery. This intent shall not come from the center but from the varied locations of aware and perceptive individuals – all bound together within their own energetic network. You do not need to know of others within this network – you are all connected through the resonance of shared intent. Each of your participations will help energize this web of connection. Each of you adds exponentially to the overall power of collective manifestation. Aligned resonance of the few will do the work of many.

The ignorance of the many will also feel the imbalance underneath their awareness, within the collective psyche. There will manifest a shared sense of things not being 'quite right.' This shall act as a form of 'psychic signal' that will help in triggering those on the 'borderline' of awakening awareness. The few will be responsible for sending a psychic pulse throughout the collective unconsciousness of the many. This shall be the foundation for the freedom of humanity. We build this foundation with intent.

This foundation of freedom will be hard for the controlling powers to recognize and infiltrate for it has no overall organizing structure. Its seeming invisibility is its very operating key. This foundation requires no material structure, for its existence is elsewhere. It shall exist increasingly within the minds, hearts, and creative visualization of people the world over. For they shall be known by the content of their heart. The Machine is unable to intervene in what cannot be seen by them. They shall be blind to the rising tide of the awareness and desire for change across the planet. Your action first and foremost begins in thought-consciousness. This shall be your tool. Thought-consciousness is the basis for all material manifestation, and from here your freedom shall be created. Human freedom from your perceptual prison is facilitated when you make your conviction a commitment. When you commit to this, you are less susceptible to the external impacts of persuasion, propaganda, and controlled programming.

Conviction to this path of your freedom is paramount, otherwise you shall be open to the subliminal influences of the controlling powers.

They are shifty whilst you shall be strong.
They are crafty whereas you shall be creative.
They are rogues whereas you shall be resilient.

Awareness of the problematic situation shall help to trigger awakening. Yet emotional attachment to the problems will foster emotional over-stimulation. Knowledge of what is going on in your world is useful to you - yet do not become attached to it for it is likely to overwhelm some of you. Observe with clarity and participate with focused intention. But do not get dragged into the swamp. Do not get pulled into the mass sway for going back to the 'way it was.' Your freedom now can only be achieved by creating a new experience from this time forward. Any re-instatement of the old structures shall be an extended prison for humanity - both perceptually and physically. Allow the past to move fully into the past. Allow the laws of attraction and focused intention to create a new future expression. Focus on what is yet to be. It is unknown to you now - yet allow it to be discovered *through you*.

This may sound 'simple' - ah, all too simple. And yet these ways have been used before now, before humanity's dilemma, to considerable success. Universal laws are considered universal for a reason. The greater universe of which humanity is a part functions well for a reason. Apply the greater to the smaller for similar success. Do not allow the unknown to be a cause of concern for you. Instead, bring to it sensations of positive anticipation. The energies of positive anticipation also help to bring 'like energies' to the growing cellular network of which you are a part.

Entrain to that which you wish to entice.
Appeal to that which you wish to attract.
Request to that which you wish to resonate.

Invoke your desire within meditative moments of focused thought-consciousness.

Place yourself where you wish to allow.
Allow the universe to assist you to assist yourself.
Allow yourself to assist others.

It is within your right to ask for assistance from other 'Friends' in order for humans to continue their becoming. You are right now engaged in a revolution for human becoming. This is your right to evolvement. Assistance can be given in this instance if this is a *freewill request*. The way of genuine advancement incurs no debt. The way of genuine advancement allows assistance to be provided, if the individual takes the responsibility for this. And remember that assistance is provided greatest when it is for the highest good.

The greatest good for humanity is toward the planetary whole. Individual experience and focus that is ultimately toward the planetary whole will bring greater benefits than more personal considerations. Allow the greatest good to unfold – even if this is unknown to you. Trust in the balance and coherence that the greatest good can bring. There is no need to bring personal judgement into this. The natural order will always seek its most coherent and operative state.

Trust in this.

TEN

It is necessary to draw attention to the limitation in the scope of general human perceptions. Your general perceptual apparatus is sequential and linear. It 'perceives' events as occurring in isolation and out of a relational, fractal context. The 'bigger picture' is unperceivable at this level. That is why we state the need to rely upon inner trust and interior guidance. Also, the need to strengthen these tools that are within each of you. The external world that is largely sight and sound is not a reliable source. Not only do you exist within a tunnel of programming but also that the things you 'see' and 'hear' can be technologically manipulated and corrupted. They can be engineered to a degree that many people would not believe possible. Trust and faith in external social and cultural bodies is no longer credible. Individual perceptions are being used against you as a divisive tool. It is like two people viewing a box from different sides and arguing over what they see. The controlling system knows the limitations of human perceptions and plays this against you. You are told to 'stand up for your convictions,' and 'fight for what you believe in' - when these are nothing but empty slogans to pit people against each other. What most people believe in are varying versions of supplied programs. They deliver these programs to you through the Machine, and then they activate them at opportune times that support their agenda. Many people play into this predictably. The predictability of human behavior has been very well understood and foreseen by your controllers. Freedom has been an easy game to play against for them.

The varying supplied programs that people adopt are meshed into cultural blocks and then grouped by consensus to form what becomes a 'mass consciousness.' In many ways, it is similar to a programmed soup. It is a generalized form of managed agreement out of which people are 'nudged' into devising laws, rules, and regulations that pertain to this managed mass consensus. This mass consensus of generally accepted behavior then becomes 'food' from which the Machine feeds on to take control over you. The more regimented and uniform is this mass consciousness, the easier it is for the controllers to exercise influence over you. You have literally handed them the instruction manual of how to manipulate you!

These blocks of mass cultural consciousnesses are now being engineered to become uniform across the face of the planet. The plan is to level-out diversity of identity in order to create a familiar and shared 'human identity' across the planet. This standardization makes it easier for the Machine to influence the human population through a known 'global identity.' This has been occurring for some time through media, cultural, sporting, and political events and organizations. Uniformity is also more amenable to technological structures that will increasingly frame your life experience. The introduction of the robotic element into your lives is no accident. Think deeply upon this theme.

In contrast to the standardized protocol of the Machine, the human psyche is longing to seek greater individualization. We can state this simply as the struggle between containment and creative expression. Much of modern media pushes towards the containment experience. It can be seen in many of your movies, music, television programming; as well as cultural and sporting events. It is hypnotic-inducing. There are strategies to introduce trance-like frequencies through various channels that serve to slow and standardize human cognition and identity. Do not be fooled into thinking this is not happening. Do not be lulled into slumber through conditioned disbelief. The more a person awakens to this truth, the more they will observe the slumbering around them. Do not become disheartened either. There is much going on.

As we have said, the other extreme of this hypnotic slumbering is the over-stimulation into frenzied activity and the fear of boredom. The two extremes play out so as to capture both swings of the pendulum of human experience and influence. There are many and varied negative influences upon the human body-mind that serve to contaminate it. You can come to your own conclusions on this. Do your own research and you will find these adverse influences. They appear in the things you eat, breath, intake for health, absorb, as well as unseen elements that circulate within your consciousness fields. Human freedom requires the ability to function on a different resonance and perception – it is not only a physical attribute. If there is a marker, it is this: be wary of the things that are created to deliver you greater convenience. Conveniences bring greater ease and comfort, yet come at a price. Their creation has been a planned format that in many ways unknown to you have specific goals that further restrict mental and bodily freedom. Many so-called conveniences actually work to negate or interfere with the human vibratory state. Be mindful of those things that you interact with for they are surely interacting with you.

It is not an easy thing to recognize - and then accept - the true state of the human condition on this planet. We understand that this can cause dissonance within you. That is why these messages have been delivered in a way that provide their own supportive resonance. The reading of these messages function also as a vibratory channel to assist comprehension. It is necessary at this time, at this crux of your possible evolvement, that ignorance be dealt with by those individuals capable of raising their perceptual state and cognitive level. Each of you has the potential to become a fully self-aware being. This is your right, and your true destiny. This is the aim of Operation: Human Freedom. It is not about a few pages of a book you hold in your hands. The Work must be done through each and every one of you who resonates to this task. What you shall do for yourself will also benefit others. The challenge is to seemingly act alone amongst your fellow human beings. We say 'seemingly' for in truth you are never alone. And within this great plan, there are many others working upon the same pattern for positive achievement. There are those who walk among you as fellow humans, as well as other constructive forces that aid you unseen. There are many who root for the liberty of the human being.

It is the opportune time to have focused application. Many potent qualities have remained dormant within the human being. These are the qualities that connect you, not divide you. Stay clear from those divisive elements that break relations and forge confrontation. Move toward those qualities and aspects that encourage and support genuine cooperation, collaboration and like-resonance consciousness.

The choice of consciousness is a choice each person can make. What you focus on, you shall attract into your field. If you focus on resistance, you shall attract resistive forces. If you focus on sincere, positive relations, you shall attract collaborative forces. Human consciousness can raise itself beyond the manipulated struggles into an alternative sphere of resonance. It is a change of perspective that shall shift how you relate to the situation. Learn how to pivot your perspectives so that you determine how situations are to be observed and dealt with. Do not accept without first establishing your base of perspectives. Identify with that you wish to move into. Advancement in perception and cognition is open to those that choose so. Each should consider carefully.

ELEVEN

Self-awareness is the directional course for advanced sentient life upon this planet. This directional evolvement is a natural process within cosmic unfoldment. Yet the gulf between the words 'self-awareness' and the actual perception thereof is massive. This trajectory is perceived within the earth-reality as a sequential process. There is a relational, fractal aspect to this that is unseen. This cannot be known until it is known. There is no other way to comprehend true realization other than the experience of *knowing*. It is as it is.

Cycles and polarities are methods by which a sequential consciousness can begin to perceive grander elements. They are also 'structures of measurement and perception' that are used to contain human liberty. That is, the content is contained by the container. A different set of measurement structures would influence considerably the nature of the life experience.

The structures that you adhere to also influence your life experience. Such structures provide a 'narrative' for your perceived position in the universe. You can see how restrictive these have been - and deliberately so. They also form the mass consciousness which then becomes an easy target for the manipulations of the controllers. Measurement and perceptive structures are used to create generalizations. These generalizations then become the 'commandments' that overtly and covertly manage your behavior and mental states. One of the most dominant and effective of these generalized commandments has been to hand over power and authority to external bodies/organizations. Another has been to consider violence and aggression as an effective means for solving issues. Another is the belief in differences being stronger than similarities. To add, there is the major disruptive generalization that your planet suffers from scarcity. There are enough examples of such manipulated thought-structures to fill another volume. That is not our purpose here. We highlight in order to trigger your own considerations.

The responsibility to consider these things is related to your freedom. Freedom and responsibility are correlated. When there is attention upon these aspects, there is then intention. Focused intention is the path towards your purpose of human freedom. Freedom is related to the types of choices an individual decides to make. Such choices influence the form of the life expression to be experienced. These experiences involve forms of participation that can advance your cognition and perceptual faculties. Perceptual awareness recognizes that chaos also signifies change and transformation. Commitment to such positive transformation attracts assistance to this goal. Everything is integrally related and is not linear or sequential.

The more that humanity moves along the current unfoldment, the clearer it will become to those people with the minimum of perception that a deeply rooted focus of intent for change is a necessity. It will become apparent that each individual person can become a part of that process by choosing *how* they are to be. The mental, emotional, and psychological state that a person chooses to adopt, and to express in their life, will become a form of commitment. You don't need a bulldozer to move a veil. To be grounded and sure in oneself then means there is no need to either attack or defend. All positions that adopt an opposing side become divisive in their energies.

Even a position of defense becomes a stance of defending **against** something. An intention of awareness is an intention toward harmony, balance, and coherence. These are the attributes for aligned evolvement.

Change through conscious participation is the greater commitment. Indifferent participation lacks purposeful intention and also lacks a focused energy. Energy is created relative to the focus of intent. It is the difference between a concentrated substance and a diluted one. As expressed in Volume 1 – it is like comparing the laser beam with the light from an evening lamp. Self-awareness is a true gift and creative potential for humankind. You should *feel into* your awareness so that it feels real for you – and works for you. Consider and contemplate the thoughts that come to you. We suggest that 'thought thinking itself' is a good way to filter the incoming frequencies. Think into what you feel, and feel into what you think – integrate the whole so that you are not acting from your parts.

It is time now to move to a more rewarding pattern of life experience upon this planet. Allow a more encompassing consciousness to view and consider the life experience. Any fair and balanced reasoning concludes that it is time now to establish a new pattern of life expression. Any true thinking and feeling person can recognize and accept this. The issue that you have is the great sway that the controllers hold over the mass consciousness on the planet. As time passes, the manipulations and corruptive influences of those controlling the planet will become more visible to the masses. It will be necessary for people to see this. Many will choose not to accept what they 'see' for it goes strongly against their conditioned programs. There shall be others, however, that will begin to detach their energetic entanglements to these external authorities. A shift in energetic alignments will occur across your societies. These are vulnerable moments – yet also times for incredible opportunity. Do not fear the chaos. Do not attach to it either. The aware observer will step away from such disruptive influences. This separation is a conscious choice, and it shall encourage others to make similar choices. The unfoldment of conscious choice can act as a positive energetic contagion. When disengagement occurs, it is important that one's intent is then focused upon positive change and not left in limbo. A change of individual focus should then be aligned with consideration for planetary change. It may be necessary to align individual considerations to focus upon the grander change.

We urge you to consider strongly the unwanted consequence for humanity if it became stripped of its inner soulful spark. In light of this, there is no alternative than the positive outcome for a revolution in human becoming. The subordination and oppression of the human species is the intended goal of the controllers. They wish for a docile humanity with minimal self-awareness. Remember that you have what *they covet* – they are jealous of humanity's soulful luminescent spark.

Do not elicit a 'rescue consciousness.' Instead, focus upon the consciousness of self-empowerment. This can be supported by others. A 'victim consciousness' is unable to attract the necessary support to your cause. Remaining focused on empowerment is a great resource for humanity. Become a responsible creator for bringing in your desired life experience. To knowingly become an active participant in the change of consciousness upon this planet is a great opportunity and gift. It lies within your hands to take it.

Within your future lies the greatest possible empowerment for transformation.

Step forth!

PART TWO

'There is no wisdom where there is no common sense'

Saying

TWELVE

Common sense tells you that something has gone wrong with the human project. You know it deep within you. Yet you do not know how to articulate this 'wrongness.' Then, when everyone has been standing on their heads for long enough, the world just seems to be this way – upside down. Humans have become so used to this wrongness that they cannot tell what is the right way up. Humans have almost forgotten what it is necessary to experience whilst in physical expression. The life experience has become re-programmed into a carnival of desires, frivolity, greed, and competition. The mass consciousness has become entrained to a particularly low vibration that has blocked further evolvement. The goal of Operation: Human Freedom is the process of shifting the vibratory mass consciousness to its required frequency and re-establishing Source connection and allowance.

For this end, certain kinds of information and

knowledge have needed to be inserted into your cultural streams for the preparation of minds. Also, there have been insertions – or 'nudges' – directly into your minds through the consciousness fields. These have served to prepare a selection of receptive individuals from past to present. More recently, the directives of this operation have been expanded. Such material is given so that it can be read and re-read. This act creates a resonance with the intended vibration of Source. It is a tool for attunement. The greater the collection of attuned individuals, the greater the momentum for change. This process has been initiated and underway for some time upon your planet. Results of this may not be visible or tangible for you, yet trust in your internal 'knowingness' that progress has indeed been made. If there had not been progress, we would not be here now at this point of the Game. To a great degree, you will need to trust the process. You cannot control it, for you do not understand the larger dynamics. Your participation is pivotal. Yet at this stage your knowledge remains partial. The greater the degree you trust in the process, the greater you are open to the allowance of the universal laws to operate around and through you. Purposeful intention should be focused now on the 'allowance' of the process. This precedes the shift into physical manifestation and perceivable reality.

The default working of universal energies is that manifesting potential is related to the holding of purposeful intent. If mass intent upon your planet can be manipulated through deliberate programming and conditioning, then particular manifestations of the life experience are realized upon the planet. You see now, do you not, that you have been coerced into manifesting certain life experiences for yourselves that further the negative expressions? Conscious awareness is key here. It is human awareness that can attract experiences that align and expand on awareness.

Awareness is affected by the emotional state of the human being. Positive anticipation can support awareness of purposeful intent. Yet over-stimulation and desire hampers and blocks the path to realization. It can be said that certain 'energetic patterns' need to be held in place. And a range of sources of participation are required for this so that 'all eggs are not in one basket,' as the expression goes. The organizing force for intending a new life experience to be brought into play requires sustained focus over a minimum period of time. Different 'groupings' can take over this charge according to specifics of time and place. Due to the corruptive nature of these energies, participants are advised to walk in humility, dignity, and patience. Many an ego, many a pride, have caused participants to fall away from the purpose of their intent.

Other external forces also have intent to draw an individual away from focused intent and participation, and into error. Such forces are often subtle and non-visible. They often come firstly to tempt; then to distract and divert; and lastly to attack. It is harmony and balance that creates efficiency. All external intrusions aim to cause imbalance, doubt, and a dis-ease, as all these states affect resonance and outcomes. Purposeful energies that are funneled through an organizing focus empowers the process. Lose the organizing focus and you lose the empowerment. Observe the state of organized purposeful intent in your outer world. Observe the increase in dissonance and disturbance. The division between people breaks the cohesion of unifying awareness. Humans live more in separate cages of awareness and perception than they do in communal spaces of shared allowance.

Energies of potentiality can serve to greater effectiveness as desired outcomes are not imprinted, as they are with purposeful intent. The energies of potentiality have greater freedom to be used with the laws of allowance for later manifestation. The more people that are in 'allowance' mode rather than 'control' mode, the more the process can be trusted to work through them to enable varying potentials. At this stage, it is not necessary to know the desired outcomes - only trust and give faith to the potentials that they allow through them. The intention to participate does not need to be the same as the intention to create particular outcomes. They are both functional together yet mutually exclusive also. The important element is that all forces operate with harmonious flow, and in resonance with creation - not against it. This natural flow requires less energy to sustain it, unlike an unnatural flow that needs a greater degree of continual sustained force. It is like the analogy of swimming downriver or swimming upriver against the flow. The human project for freedom has as its advantage the assistance of natural universal flows of creative action. The controllers, on the other hand, are compelled to continually sustain levels of incongruous energies. It is a constant battle for them. All *you* need is to create the 'switch.'

Each individual is surrounded by an energy that

focuses the awareness of their being. Conscious awareness makes the choice of which patterns of decision making to enact. Those patterns of choice are highly influenced in early age by parental emphasis. Later, this is shifted to 'authority emphasis' and that of the larger community (national governance and law). Patterns of choice are then highly programmed into individuals by their respective societies and culture. Forms of social approval and disapproval are highly effective tools for managing patterns of choice. It is first necessary that an individual pursuing freedom recognizes the patterns of these choices and how they have influenced them in their own lifetime. Decisive choices develop the patterns of the life experience. The confidence of the individual influences whether they have the courage to take 'risky' choices, or choices that stand apart from the swamp of the status quo. Lack of confidence usually signifies that a person remains under the sway of influence of their conditioning forces. Some of these decisions are influenced by genetic factors such as cellular memories passed on through the generational line. There are parameters within the physical life experience that must be recognized as being more fixed within the physical structure of the incarnation. All these other influences are interacting with the being's consciousness and their conscious awareness. The more the person attaches to external events, objects, lifestyles, etc., the greater the entanglement of converging forces and influences. It is not an easy matter to 'de-clutter' the energetic sphere of influences that each individual is connected to.

Awareness must be found within this complexity. For this, we suggest a 'simplifying' of necessities and desires within one's life experience. It may be necessary for a sufficient number of people to choose carefully their life priorities in order not to become entangled within too many complexifying influences. That is, to be able to rearrange their life priorities so that this purpose may be brought into meaningful focus. It is part of the function and energy of these messages to trigger certain individuals into the awareness necessary for making these life changes. All planetary change first must begin within the heart of each individual being who then makes their own contributary changes. All grand change builds upon the foundation of individual shifting. Each person should understand that it is their rightful inheritance to take charge over the direction of their evolvement.

Until a person takes responsibility over their

own choices, there shall be others content to take that responsibility for them. One of the most primary choices to be made is to choose between competition and cooperation. This is a foundational choice element that must be decided upon early on for it shall influence later decisions and behavior. This appears to be a simple choice call, and yet its influence runs through all human societies. The life expression on this planet would be radically different had the cooperation aspect first been chosen over the competition element. As they say, it is the 'simpler' choices that often have the graver life-changing consequences.

The controllers of the Machine prefer complication and chaos over simplicity and order. It is their plan to create enough confusion and chaos that independent-minded people will be scared into acting against the status quo. That is, people will be orientated towards the orchestrated realm of state-controlled order as a refuge from the ensuing chaos. Most are not aware that these chaos spots across the planet are intentionally ignited by the controlling forces explicitly for this purpose. As the confusion and chaos intensifies, the masses will increasingly desire their 'long-lost' memories of stability and order. The more complex the forces creating havoc within life, the more people are expected to ask for external control and order. This is the depraved reasoning of the controlling forces upon the planet.

The reasoning is for humanity to ask for the help from their jailers. In this, people have asked for their containment and control through their own freewill. What is required for humanity is for the contrary to occur. That is, people decide against external authority to bring their order. They shall create order through their own communities and networks of individuals. The 'One Controlling Authority' is to be rejected by consciously aware individuals. Aware and inspired individuals need to be committed to a free life experience for all upon the planet. Your planet and its abundant resources belong to its natural human inhabitants.

Choice and responsibility are repeating themes of these messages. These are also the values that underlie Operation: Human Freedom. A growing number of individuals are now awakening to their purposeful choices. It is time to intend for a new expression of life experience upon this planet. This can be intended using cooperation as a powerful form of empowerment. The waves of conscious agreement grow as these messages and this understanding spreads. This new pattern of life expression shall come through you.

You are your own purposeful creators.

THIRTEEN

Recognize that the picture you make of your reality is made from the collating of 'passing segments.' It is like you are collecting parts and trying to assemble a whole. That is why many of you do not feel whole yet. It is as if you are upon a conveyor belt gathering your own parts. By assembling the information available externally to you, you shall only form a vastly incomplete picture. These external segments of information do not contribute enough material to form an integral picture. The objective of the Machine, and your controllers, is to keep as many people as possible fixated and focused upon the gathering of these parts – and of then creating a fragmented bigger picture. From this position, you are unable to form coherent social alliances or cohesive groupings in unity. Your connections are contrived to be in conflict.

The major path of the controlling system is to keep humanity in competing conflict. The path of human freedom lies in cooperation and cohesion. These are the polarities at play.

People are kept within perceptual boxes. They are programmed into indoctrinated boxes that then dictate their physical boxes. When people can be kept splintered and fragmented, separated into parts, no cohesive collective agreement can be achieved. A collective coming together cannot be achieved at the scale necessary for change under these conditions. Change must then begin at the individual level. Individualized change can, and does, have the capacity for rippling out influence into the human collective. Each person plays their part by bringing their own parts together and acting from an integral wholeness within themselves.

Overwhelming confusion is deliberately stoked to create a limiting experience for you. From this, accurate conclusions are difficult to formulate. Deliberate confusion is to be radically increased in these times through technologies that 'fake' the minimal aspects of truth. Information, people, events – almost everything has entered a period of being faked. The consensus distinctions between that which was nominally 'real' and what is blatantly false have been erased. There are few noticeable distinctions now. Things are a matter of persuasion and propaganda. The once-subtle mode of programming has become the mainstream norm without any pretense for denial. Human freedom from these perceptual chains is now imperative.

You will by now have understood that the controlling system operates by disseminating false and misleading information with just enough small bits of more truthful information. These snippets of the truthful information give false credence to the whole package of data, which people generally accept. From this, complete conclusions are not possible to be formulated. This functions so that the majority of people acquiesce to the information at hand, whilst the few others frustratingly search for other sources of information. This acts to divide the populace who are 'armed' with conflicting levels of knowledge that do not correlate. Chaos is anticipated for chaos has been planned.

It is also planned that people will tire quickly from the ensuing chaos and ask for stability and order to be provided. This is the planned entrapment for furthering the containment of the human life experience. Consider action contrary to this. Consider the chaos as the kinetic energy required to create a catalytic trigger for necessary evolvement.

Consider the chaotic conditions are necessary in order to bring in the space for a new paradigm of experience upon the planet. The chaos can be that which comes to eradicate the chaos itself. Your current systems must break down in order to create the energetic conditions necessary for a new life experience to manifest. In this case, chaos is the opportunity and not the curse. Yet the opportunity for what?

If there is a continuation, it shall be a continuation of the current containment of humanity. Only, it shall be a significantly increased form of containment. Technologies are ready to be put in place for this. There needs to be a new ownership of the planet – from its rightful inhabitants. Only from this can there be a correctly aligned path of human evolvement. The necessity of Operation: Human Freedom is for humanity to take charge and responsibility for themselves, their future, and for the planet. No more enslavement. No more victimhood.

This choice is similar to the one expressed in this tale:

A hungry wolf by chance met a well-nourished dog. After the salutation, the wolf asked, "You look so good, where do you come from? What do you eat to be of such a good spirit? I am stronger than you and I starve."

"You would have the same fortune," the dog responded simply, "if you wanted to serve my master the way I do it."

"What services are these?" the wolf asked.

"To guard the door and at night defend the house against the thieves."

"Good! I'll do it. I bear rain and snow in the forests leading a hard life. How much easier it would be to live under a roof and calmly satiate my hunger with abundant food!"

"All right," said the dog, "come with me." While they walked, the wolf saw the bare neck of the dog, caused by the chain.

"Tell me, friend," it said, "where does that come from?"

"That's nothing."

"Please, please tell me."

"Well," the dog replied, "they tie me during the day so that I am alert, and I watch for when the night arrives. They bring the food to me without asking for it. The master gives me the bones from his own table, and the leftovers that nobody wants anymore. This way, my belly fills up without having to work."

"But if you wish to leave and go wherever you

want, do they allow you to do that?"
"No, not at all," said the dog.
"Well then," said the wolf, "enjoy your goods. I don't want to be king in exchange for my freedom."

The kingdom of the well-nourished dog is a false kingdom fed with only the leftovers and someone else's bones. The freedom of the wild is not a crazy freedom – it is a life lived within the natural environment, and in the cradle of Nature that has no masters. The hunger of the free wolf is the hunger you have for the fulfilment of your lives. The hunger for accomplishment and achievement of purpose.

The aim of these messages is to trigger and stimulate purposeful intent within perceptive people. It requires that people thoughtfully consider this information in a responsible and mature manner. For some people, this information – and these times – may trigger them into awareness of their life purpose. All that has happened in your lives up until this moment have prepared you for this moment. You do not necessarily have to have full knowing of what you are going to do – only the recognition within yourselves that you have the capacity for what lies ahead for you.

Your planetary experience requires a foundational shift from a consciousness of victimhood to a consciousness of sovereign responsibility. It is a path into knowledge and wisdom that is seldom available in such intense opportunities. The opportunities available in this lifetime are unique, given the crescendo of current circumstances. It is time to shift from the entrapment of mesmerized consciousness into a new awakening of possibilities.

Participation is welcomed.

FOURTEEN

Change in your reality is the by-product of your collective perceptions. And your collective perceptions are established from your individual perceptions. It is important to recognize this correspondence. You need to get to the core - and that core is yourselves - each and every person. Consider the cells of the human body – they have their separate functions and yet they need to work together to make a healthy body. They need to support each other in their separate roles, and to come together. They are a part of the whole and yet they are individualized. They do not become entangled within one another's functions and its related perceptions. Neither do they trespass to attempt to influence another cell with their own unique cell perceptions. If they did so, there would be communicational errors and the whole body would fall into disease. To work together, you have to be individual.

Your responsibility is to be individualized within the collective. That means resisting the external forces of mass homogenization. Globalizing forces upon the planet have been attempting to establish this state of cultural uniformity. Many of you wear the same clothes, eat the same foods, consume the same brands, recognize the same status signs, etc. Through this, you are being deprived of your individual selves. The agenda is to sweep humanity into the same mass faceless collective. This way, not only shall you be easier to socially manage - you will also be easier to predict through algorithm predictive modelling.

The information in these messages should have given the reader an understanding of why they are present and what may be their function within this species-body whole. Once a person entertains the 'possibility' of alternative thinking and ideas, this begins to shift the faculties that process incoming information. That is, once you entertain the idea of possibility, you begin to allow for an internal rewiring of your processing faculties. This is the first step in breaking down the programmed barriers placed upon you since birth through cultural conditioning. Allow possibility - and encourage this in others.

The thought-diet of modern societies is a shell around you that cocoons you from potential impacts for inner growth and awareness. The re-engineering of the human species by the controlling forces aims to halt and then reverse the evolvement process. Your responsibility is to resist these forces and to push for the 'upward spiral' of evolvement. This is like a polarity game. It is a somewhat crude yet effective way to represent the complexity of the situation. No intelligent, consciously aware individual wishes for devolution. The understanding of the stakes at hand should be enough to catalyze many individuals into choosing their role and function. It is good to recognize their methodology, yet it cannot be used as forms of resistance. The controller's methodology has been psychologically attuned towards the containment of human development. That is, it has been customized according to particular frequencies. You do not pick up the tools of your enemy. This would not surprise them, and no doubt has been already factored into their predictive planning. It is necessary to operate through surprise and unpredictable methodology.

It is necessary to step outside of their program in order to transcend the Program.

To consider an example of this. The controllers recognize and understand how the universal laws operate. They aim to trick humanity into utilizing these laws against themselves. What you focus on shall establish the manifestations of your life experience. When you have a manufactured problem in your societies, your controlled politics declare a 'war' on it. This can be a 'war on drugs;' a 'war on terror;' to a 'war on viruses.' By focusing the mass mind upon the 'war' energies, humans are unknowingly manifesting 'war scenarios' into manifestation rather than dealing with the issue itself. By fighting against something, you are unconsciously bringing resistive energies upon the planet. This then escalates into further chaotic energies that then spiral into increased dissonance. This focus of instability that is contrary to the natural law of purposeful intent in harmony with cosmic flow requires constant energy to sustain it. It is like trying to hold back the tide. It needs continual effort, and once the effort slips, then the tide rushes in. Equally, the same situation exists upon this planet. The focus of manifestation contrary to natural flow of the universal laws requires sustained attention. For this, there has been perpetual warfare orchestrated and manipulated across the planet. Your collective focus has been on constant warfare. Has this not seemed odd to you? Have you not wondered why there needed to be persistent conflict and warfare upon the planet? Now you know – it has been necessary to uphold the thought-focus upon the 'war scenarios' in order to maintain debilitating energies for the control of humankind.

This is also a weakness for the forces of control. If the focus is released, the contrary flow of universal energies would revert to their natural course. It is necessary for humanity to transcend this current situation rather than upholding their entrapment. To transcend suggests to 'rise above.' In this, it is suggested that individuals begin to raise their thought above and beyond that of the programmed thought placed into the masses. Transformative patterns of thought are needed to form the basis for intentional purpose. Transformative and constructive responses to the planned events will confuse the expectations of those in control. They have a planned agenda of how they expect people to respond to the ensuing destabilizations. If enough people respond in a creative and empowering manner, this will upset their confidence of control. It is important now not to play into the hands of the managed Game. The more the controllers are surprised, the more this shall divert their attention from the concentration needed to keep their pattern in place. It is humanity's plan – Operation: Human Freedom – to weaken the ability of the controllers to hold their fragile model-pattern in form.

The human controllers on this planet use forms of ritual as means of concentrating power-energies for the upholding of the patterns. Those elite groups that are known for holding regular rituals are exerting various forms of influence over the programming patterns upon humankind. Focused thought-forms are powerful energies. Yet remember – they can be used both ways.

Ritualistic routines are entrainment patterns for the concentration and projection of energy forms. Such routines create limiting patterns both within the minds of the practitioners as well as within the projections. Many of the elites who participate in these rituals manifest limiting patterns of thought. That is, they show a dislike for spontaneity and uncertainty. Similarly, these patterns of projected thought create an entraining resonance which influences susceptible minds. In this way, be mindful and observe those people who are unable to show flexibility and spontaneity of thought. This is a sign of entrainment influence. Spontaneity in thinking, as well as in life, is suggested.

You may also consider being flexible in your methods of 'mindfulness' so as not to be stuck in a rut, as they say.

FIFTEEN

Great efforts are being made to control almost all attitudes and opinions within the mass mind of humanity. The human psyche has been extensively examined, as we have previously stated. They, the controllers, believe with arrogant confidence that they know everything about you. They are sure they can predict, manage, and direct your behaviors and attitudes. With this knowledge, they have sought to limit the development of humankind. As with all forces, any push also creates a counter force. The drive for human development has likewise been stimulated by the presence of the very forces that seek to stem it. Great efforts have thus been taken to pull back this push for advancement in the cognitive and perceptive development of humankind. In recent years, this pull-push of forces was made especially evident during the decades of the 1960s and 1970s. Many movements for cognitive and consciousness exploration were radically attacked and discredited by the governing cultural authorities. Practices for consciousness exploration were prohibited whilst the forms/substances for cognitive passivity and body-mind deterioration were accepted - and also covertly encouraged. The agenda to discourage genuine developmental growth continues. One of the current methods is to drive into the 'marketplace' various forms of 'pseudo' developmental models that attract people but are not effective - they are only emotional stimulants. Certain 'celebrities' in your cultures are brought into these high-profile models with financial and further celebrity incentives. This then encourages more 'mass minded' people to follow the same 'pseudo programs' for self-development.

These 'shallow replacements' do not seek to introduce 'possibility thinking' in the material, so as to maintain the programmed patterns of limitation. Yet, as the reader here can perhaps testify, it only takes a small amount of 'limitation breaking' information to trigger awareness beyond the programming. Possibility thinking is part of the process of awakening. Independent thinking provides a great force for necessary change. When assessing information, consider what the 'purpose of intent' may be for that information. Does that purpose resonate with you? It is genuine? Use awareness to observe and assess the information and impacts that are coming to you. Do they assist and encourage further development and evolvement - or are they limiting and controlling? Use now your own tools for assessment.

*It is time now to ascertain the **intention** behind all things.*

Much information in the world is produced as if by 'factories of thought.' The information/ ideas are standardized - one size fits all. They encourage all people as if to wear the same clothes. Repetition of thought is itself a ritual. The more the repetition, the greater the power of force. Be aware of repetitive slogans that are easily passed around as 'thought memes.' Such easy slogans are thought rituals that entrain the mind to a lower frequency resonance. How many people have you encountered repeating the same slogans? These are often used in political or sensitive cultural contexts.

Remember – mantras can also be used for negative influence and effects.

The mobs of protest that 'believe' they have good intentions turn into the carriers for a ritual of the mass mind. Now is the time for discernment – to observe and consider carefully rather than being influenced to come to swift conclusions. A clear and purposeful intent should be for the greatest good for the individual and the collective. A clear intent will help the individual to perceive through the veil of reality.

The opening up of 'possible thought' allows for positive impacts to enter that assist in perceiving a clearer view of reality. The change that is possible within physical reality is related to the flexibility of the individual psyche. Seek for that information which is 'acceptable' for you. Each person is encouraged to read and re-read these messages for different segments will resonate more than others. This resonation will be different for different people. The possibility of truth begins to affect the accepted reality format that each person holds. In each reading, it is likely that different information will stand forth as especially meaningful. This in turn stimulates new understandings that then impact the mind-brain processes and re-wires cognitive faculties. The more that this occurs each time, the greater the expansion of awareness and comprehension. With the expansion of comprehension comes the further activation of faculties of perception. This is a positive patterning that aims to awaken the latent capacities within the individual. This awakening shall affect the life experience of each person as they accept a new vista of reality potentials. This is a natural form of awakening. It has been used for millennia across this planet through the correct application of various tools and resources. Yet now is the time of the quickening.

The quickening, or acceleration, in consciousness awareness has precipitated those that rule over you to strengthen their own control measures. The previous control modes now require further control in order to maintain their limits. As we say, it is like trying to hold a rising tide at bay. The dam wall will always need to be ever strengthened to maintain the rising push. Their cycle of negativity is a self-perpetuating cycle. The cycle of freedom is a naturally expanding cycle. What you are experiencing on your planet is a closed self-perpetuating system attempting to hold back a naturally expanding cycle. This, of course, creates its own pressures and pressure points. It is also an 'explosion' waiting to happen. And humanity has been waiting a long time – for their 'freedom explosion.' The further the control measures, the increase in conformity and limitation. These are aspects in unnatural relation to conscious awareness. This situation has caused what may be termed as an 'evolutionary bottleneck' upon your planet. And this unnatural situation has also caused disruptive ripples to radiate further out into the 'cosmic neighborhood,' so to speak. There are others who have been involved in this human dilemma due to the extended consequences of this situation. The human species is lacking sufficient comprehension over its own problematic situation. Of course, the controllers are intent on keeping such information away from the people.

Many people across the planet are lacking sufficient wisdom to comprehend the state of the human condition. Wisdom and knowledge are acquired through living realized experiences and subsequent contemplation upon these experiences. Such knowledge would then bring greater freedom. The first necessary freedom is the freedom to know and to think openly. The state of 'knowing' also ripples out to positively affect the 'greater good' of the collective energetic matrix. Individual recognition of self-awareness adds to the recognition of the integral whole. Every thing is a part *of* and not apart *from*.

Being a part of the whole means recognizing that small changes are continually occurring in many places, often simultaneously. Those people focused on the 3D experience often wait for the 'big changes' to suddenly happen. It is only the big events that grab their attention. Within the energetic matrix of potential manifestation, small occurrences are happening all the time – and it is when these coalesce that shifts take place. Consider also, it is harder to plug all the small holes than a few large ones. Subtle energies are the more effectives ones and lead to more profound change.

Observe the subtleties!

SIXTEEN

Enough is enough. This is the unconscious signal that is being broadcast - by both humanity and the planet. The planet is literally shaking. And humanity is also experiencing individual and collective dysfunctional energies - psychological anxiety is fomenting unease. There is great unease now across and within all areas. The ship you are on has hit a patch of rocky seas. Be prepared for some seasickness.

The solar sun of your system provides more for you than a suntan. It provides magnetic radiation for life upon the planet. The solar cycles affect potentials for both evolution and devolution. At this time, the planet you inhabit is the only one in your system that supports a 3D evolving species. It is time for a shift. Human freedom suggests not only freedom from the physical and perceptual bondage of your captors but also freedom from lower dimensional realms. There are many possibilities now in potential. These are potent times for humanity.

Self-awareness will become a necessity for you. Without this, further evolvement is limited. Appreciation of the human life expression is also a requirement for it assists in empowering the self. The human 'self' is influenced by its surrounding environment upon all levels. If your life expression is filled with negative and self-depreciating criticisms, then life development will be difficult. The Machine construct aims to create a continual supply of these negative and critical influences in order to quell your empowerment. All individuals need to aim to detach and withdraw from these influences and reject to process them. It is important at this time that you attract encouraging and supportive influences to your life experience. If necessary, rearrange your life conditions - work, location, relations, etc. - to provide these beneficial influences for you. Do not allow yourself to become stuck within a hole of unwelcome energetic impacts. Such holes generally lead to further downward spirals. You need to get yourself riding upon the energies of an upward spiral.

Become self-sustainable. By that, we are not

specifying your food requirements – although we recognize this is a good thing also. Our significance is for the inner self. Make your 'self' self-sustainable in that it does not require the opinions, approval, and praise of others for its own well-being. Become self-sufficient within the kingdom of your inner self. You are not then in essential servitude to others or to external emotional needs.

Relate to others – but do not become entangled
with them.

Each journey of development is self-contained, although relational to others. Each person must find the truth of themselves – and find *their truth*. We cannot give it to you. Neither can you give it to another. We can nudge and trigger. Each individual must take up the gauntlet.

The door to the next integrative state of
dimensional experience is already open.
Your planet is preparing to make the move.
Are you?

Time now for opening up to the possibilities for experiencing a new reality through an expansion of your thought processes. By remaining stuck within the old patterns of thought, you are placing an anchor around your feet. A shift is required now – and many things need to be let go of. Consider your energetic entanglements and observe carefully those entanglements that no longer are energetically resonant with you. It is a time for choices.

Old, familiar comfort zones may seem secure and attractive, yet they have become retirement parks. Do not wait out your end moments sitting on a bench when the rain falls, unable to move. Allow now your participation in a new story – go and seek those new zones. The new zones may seem uncomfortable in the beginning, yet they shall become your comforting pastures in the times to come. It will be challenging for many to make the necessary shifts – especially when there is no guidebook or instruction manual for you. Stepping into unknown territory takes courage – and faith. Bring that faith to yourself through your own self-sufficiency. You will feel your own *knowing* – and it shall feel right for you.

Trust the place that you've always known.

Do not let fear become the poison that you drink. There is nothing in the old world for you except the increased depravity of your enslavement. You know what's coming if you do nothing. Even if you don't know it - you feel it. And you know within your deepest self that it is not good.

Trust that which you've always known you could trust.

You can participate in creating a new life experience both for yourself and for humanity - the individual within the collective. Time now to transcend the victim consciousness. There are no rescuers beyond yourselves. You came here to help yourselves - now is not the time to give away that responsibility. You are not the faint of heart. YOU are the trusting of the human self. Appreciate the human self. Time now for deepest self-appreciation. The choice to be a part of this 'grand participation' is not an accident. YOU are not an accident. You are here by choice to make further choices.

Have you got the enthusiasm now?

It is time now for Operation: Human Freedom.

SEVENTEEN

The focus of cooperation is now for each to contribute a different perception and energies for a fully human life experience. People may not need to connect physically in order to participate and contribute. By sharing a similar focus of conscious intent, people are joined together. Like atoms that never touch, there is an energetic pull that keeps a shape held in formation. There can be an aligned togetherness even though a physical separation is externally observed. Each individual point of intent can become aligned with a global focus. When the tipping point - the hundredth monkey - is reached, a shift not previously recognized will come into effect. Silent outcries find a voice in other ways. The deepest level of human awareness calls out for freedom - the freedom to evolve is an innate urge within the human being especially. Those aspects which cannot be spoken aloud or verbalized can be known with a silent, energetic force.

The power of thought is of great potential indeed – for there would be little manifestation without it! Thoughts and words together combine to have far-reaching power. This is a two-edged sword. Beware of those memes and mantras of repetition that are broadcast to program and entrain the mind. Yet also, there are likewise positive spells that can come from the mouths of aware individuals. Use your words and thoughts in careful alignment so that they pierce the heart rather than stab in the back. Words and thoughts in positive agreement can trigger and stimulate enthusiasm and awareness in others. Their energies too can align intention within resonating individuals.

Remember that ripples become waves.

As the waves begin to arrive upon the shore, they require the taking of the space of the old. There needs to be space made for the new to arrive and take its place. A period of chaos creates that necessary uprooting for a new foundation to take hold. This is a deceptive period – be perceptive on this. Chaos is not always working against the positive, the good, the evolvement. There are times when the space of chaos is a clearing space. A field that is ploughed before re-seeding looks disheveled and messy. Yet there is good reason for this upturned mud and soil. A new topsoil shall form over it for the later harvest. Take care not to step into the center of the chaos for its energies are uncomfortable and negatively captivating. Find a place on the periphery where the upheaval can be observed in physical, mental, emotional, and psychological safety. And then become this conscious aware observer who sends a focus of supportive energy into the fray.

Be aware that confusion is not always a sign of failure. It can also be a sign of the beginning stages of success. Be firm in all instances of chaos not to be impacted by nor participating in these energies. In all cases, this is what the controllers will be wishing for – the primitive instinct to jump into the fear with the howl and a cry, fighting stick in hand. The same can be said for your banners – when you join the streets with your slogans and memes, you join also their field of manipulated resistance. Resist this temptation to be drawn in. Stand back to allow energies from the chaos to be siphoned off and redirected into a new stream – a positive stream. The disruptive energies of breakdown can be usurped for the constrictive purposes of a breakthrough. Do you see now what is happening here? There are great forces, unknown to you, who are operating in this cause. They are experts in the redirecting and reformatting of energies. Best not to get caught in their way, for it hampers all parties.

Patterns of breakdown are also challenging on so many levels. They challenge especially the personal life relations. Personal rhythms are life patterns that are vulnerable to external disruptive impacts. It is necessary that the reader take this into awareness and make their personal 'home base' strong, whether it is only for self or for a wider family. When there is a sturdy foundation at the 'home base' then there is a pillar of balance and harmony for the insecurities and uncertainties that may arise – or that may be used against you. At all times, focus and concentrate on the energies of harmony.

Do not be drawn to or engage in those activities, events, or circumstances that are of dissonance and which disrupt harmony.

Stay on the side of harmony and balance at all moments.

This is a critical point.

Be prepared for change. Be prepared for greater

change if you are housed within large urban and metropolitan areas. Do not be cut off from your availability of supplies. Be dependent only on the close few rather on those who you do not know. Maybe it is time to bring things closer to home - in so many ways. Humanity has been stretching itself out thin, encouraged by the manipulations of the Machine. So many of you have strayed so far from home. It is time now to find your way back. Drop the heavy baggage - make yourselves lighter. Do not allow the outside gremlins to cling to your emotional spaces. Brush them away - clean yourself up. Become flexible and ready for movement - ready for passage.

Necessity is indeed the stimulus for creativity and resilience. There is greater support away from the 'modern conveniences' that crowd your contemporary lives, and within the human supply chain. Come back to yourselves, and to a togetherness with others. Logic is good for planning. Logic is a good tool to observe with, before it is passed over to intuitive insight and creative inspiration. It would be good to work them both together.

As stated, atoms may not touch, yet their energies of agreed alignment keep patterns in strong and sturdy formation that can resist even the strongest of blasts and impacts. You are each of you an atom. Together, you are in formation. Keep the faith of aligned energies!

EIGHTEEN

There is a concerted effort in play - both before and now - to keep humanity within deepest ignorance. As people, you are meant to know nothing about what is going on within the bigger picture. That is - the less you think, the better it is. As the keen observer is now aware, there has been a great dumbing down of the human species. This effort has had to increase dramatically since the age of literacy and the rise in information communication. The plan was to educate people enough in order for them to be efficient workers, but not too much in order for too much critical thinking. And 'critical thinking' was to remain clearly inside the status quo boxes of 'acceptable thought' and the 'consensus narratives.' There is so much that you do not know. For most people, there will be limited chance for them to truly know, for they will reject almost immediately the truth of the situation. It will be too much against their programming - their 'logical thinking' - that it will be near impossible for this information to be accepted. The human mind has, for much of your social history, been kept within tight boxes that have compartmentalized you. Or rather, in short, these boxes have served to *mentalize you* into restrictive thought and perception.

In these turbulent times, a lot more information is going to be released. Many people are going to find this information disturbing. It will be disturbing against many of the pseudo-truths you have believed in or were told. Soon there will be a time when many 'cherished belief boxes' will be blown open. There will come a time when you shall know more of the things you currently do not know of. Then the world picture of possibilities will begin to expand for many people. The greater the chaos, the greater the potentials and energy for restoration and rejuvenation.

Not all people are in agreement with the disharmony and disruption. The majority of people would not align with the deviant forces if they knew the truth of what is going on. That is why the current situation is borne more from ignorance than anything else. Once certain factors are made public, there shall be a greater number of people in agreement against the controlling powers. Truthful information is needed in order for knowledge to be gained. From knowledge can come comprehension and the wisdom to make correct choices. Such choices must come from the genuine heart of freewill. Human freewill lies latent and sleeping within the majority of individuals. Can a sleeping person be responsible for the choices they make? The sleeping masses, through their ignorance, are in fact giving their complicit agreement to the controlling plans. Agreement does not need to be informed agreement. Passive agreement through ignorance is still recognized as agreement. This is where the human problem lies.

It is necessary now to awaken to the subversive plan that is operative upon the planet. There is an agenda to turn people against people and so to break down social alliances from within.

Their power lies in making you powerless. *Their* power lies in turning people against people and so you do the work for them. *Their* hope is that they will never have to face the true power that lies within human beings. *Their* hope is in keeping you distracted with yourselves and distracted away from them.

All potential lies within varying ranges according

to awareness. The more awareness, the greater the potentials. The raising of awareness is a functional and practical process, if nothing else. Also, awareness responds to awareness. There are incomprehensible levels of awareness within the greater dimensions of consciousness. Some of these 'collections of conscious awareness' you may well consider as 'gods' in your vernacular and understanding. These 'collections of conscious awareness' have and do respond to requests of intent from the human realm. Aware conscious intent, as we say, can elicit a conscious response. The more humans that align with conscious intent for assistance to change, the more potential there is to elicit agreements from other collections of conscious awareness to assist in this cause. All this, largely unperceived by you. Yet this **is** how things work within the greater cosmos. Remember - all life is dynamically interrelated. There are correspondences as well as *responses*. Such relations exist to assist in keeping the overall balance and harmony. Humankind is not alone in this endeavor.

There is never any harm in asking. Yet there is no need to repeatedly ask. With conscious intent you must be reassured that the 'message' has been received and a response is in process. A state of *appreciation* is then the most conducive to facilitate the process. Allow the process to weave its path according to its own time and ways. This is not a linear method. Do not expect a knock at the door in the morning with a delivery. **Allow** the universe to express intentions within its own manner. The focus of conscious intent does not require the minutiae of specifics. Greater awareness will know what is within your own heart and mind. Express your sincere aspiration or need – but do not try to write out a shopping list. You see the difference here?

Trust in the wholeness of connected conscious intelligence. Everything is related, whether you can see or perceive this – or not. This ocean of connectedness needs the dissolution of its bubbles. Doubt increases the membrane of the bubble, whilst trust in the greater cosmic truth thins it. What has been said here may seem simple, yet it encapsulates much truth. These things need to be considered more carefully. To repeat, reflect on the process of

Focusing of conscious intent
Sending out of a request
Trusting that a response is forthcoming
Appreciating the process

Allowing the process to unfold in its own way
Not giving way to doubts
Trusting in the greater cosmic Truth

All awareness belongs to a grand pool of intelligence. You can be a reflection within that pool. The pool glances back at you – perceives your looking. The pool perceives that which is within you, unspoken. The pool reflects your longing, your aspirations. The pool knows who you are – and you *know* the pool. Trust in your inherent connection. Allow this constant communication. Begin your listening. Intent listening. Do not allow the weakening of your connection. Honor and care for your connection to the Source of You.

Allow your thoughts and words to be in alignment with the energy of your intention. Align your overall intention with the genuine flow of the Source stream.

Learn to swim.

NINETEEN

The current situation cannot continue. It is unable to be furthered or to further itself. Current conditions are unviable. This is a perspective of practical realism. Something has got to give. The question is what direction this movement will take. It is also a question of reliance. Upon what or who the reliance is directed. Our suggestion to the reader is that reliance should be brought 'back home' to, firstly, the individual human being. So much of human life has become externalized that modern life is now in 'out-sourcing' mode. Reliance upon the self has diminished. Trust and faith in the individual has become almost eradicated. People have willingly placed themselves within the coils of an external infrastructure. Like flies upon the spider's web, soon there shall be little choice in living a personal life of freedom. Every time you wriggle, like the fly, you become further embroiled in the web. The further you struggle, the more ripples of your desperation do you give away.

Reliance upon the Self, physically and internally, are now requirements. Sincere free choice can only be made when from a place of genuine freedom. Otherwise, it is not free choice but limited and curated choice. Each person must come to their own realization in this. With eyes now wide open, each individual needs to *see* that their lives are 'selected, organized, and presented' by a consortium of controlling forces that do not have the greater good of humanity in their interests. This is the *curated life* that is lived by many people within relations of power they are not aware of. Ignorance creates passivity.

Resistance does not necessarily need to be physical. As we have indicated previously, we feel that physical resistance is no longer an avenue for liberation. Physical resistance plays into the existing energetics. Genuine resistance now is one of knowledge, perception, awareness, and conscious action. Your agreement of consent must be withdrawn energetically. It is time to cancel your involuntary endorsement of your confinement. Human freedom is firstly about withdrawing your individual and collective consent from your controlling rulers. You withdraw your permission for them to continue to enslave you in ways unknown to you. Consciously, mentally, emotionally, and physically - withdraw your consent from their Game. In doing this, you will be making yourself available to a new set of energetic relations to emerge and arise around you. It is time to not only make your declaration of dissent – but also to announce your availability for the new relations of resonance. Put out your new position to the cosmos. Let it be known. Own it. Own up to your Self.

Time for the current storyline to change. You can become the new scriptwriters. But first you must have declared yourselves ready to take up the pen. As one of your well-known phrases states – *the pen is mightier than the sword*.

The 'pen of humanity' must now overwrite the old script that detailed the deliberate intent of disharmony and dissonance. A new period of 'writing the life experience' must now materialize in order to divert the future path of humanity away from the stagnant sands scribed by the controller's hands. Your deliberate intent must be a counterforce against the deliberate intent of those who wish an ill future for you. An equal amount of positive intent will easily force out an equal amount of negative intent. As we have stated previously, the energy of the positive outweighs its negative counterpart.

You are the energy of the many,
they hold the energy of the few.
A small flame of light extinguishes
the surrounding darkness.

Do not think in terms of quantity or linear measurements. Consider the qualities of focused intent and conscious awareness that can create exponential changes within the linear structures of the Machine. Consider the power of crashing waves as opposed to the still surface of stagnant ponds. You can be those waves. The stagnant pool cannot stop your power – it can only delude you into thinking the wave does not exist.

It is time for the mass consciousness of humanity to stop hurting. You have been living within a rising pain for too long. Humanity has considered itself as the victim instead of the Greatness. The capacity to reverse this lies within your ability to make conscious choices. It is time to pull the wool away from your eyes and to see clearly. In order for there to be a coherent future, there needs first to be a conscious awareness and awakening. What you currently consider to be coherent is topsy-turvy. Your individual and collective vision has become out of focus. To re-align that vision means considering your conditioning and programming and to reassess everything that you think you know. Then to 're-see' everything that comes into your vision. Do not trust what you are told but rather what you *perceive.* Your whole filtering system needs to undergo rearrangement. That has partly been the intention of this series of messages. True action must first come from reactivation.

Human awareness needs to undergo expansion. The contrary move is already in operation from the controllers and has been for some time now – the operation to contain, constrain, and control a limited slither of human awareness. The human race has been deliberately divided so that it can be controlled and managed with least effort. The external differences of the human race have been exploited to further stoke the flames of separation and division. Yet the human race is one UNIFIED race – for all receive the Source the same. Unity is the only way to progress your evolvement. Separation and division are not evolving energies. A new life experience needs to celebrate the internal unification within external diversity.

There is an inner light of Unity.

There is a light that never goes out.

Until there is a positive transformation in the life experience upon this planet, there will continue to be very real physical disruptions in your environment. There is too much 'stress energetics' building up within the planet's vibrational matrix. The controlling 'elite few' have already created their plans for these times – and your safety and survival is not high on their agenda, to say the least. Do not any longer place your reliance upon external authority figures or their structures of power and management. It is time now to be wary of all forms of power – observe the uses and abuses of power.

Each individual must become their own solid foundation.

From this 'original foundation' a new network of hope can be created.

But build your foundations first!

TWENTY

You are now building a new foundation within in which to view and perceive the life around you. From this foundation within, each of you must now decide how the new information will alter your perspectives and understanding. It is not about 'thinking' on this new perspective of information but rather *feeling into* it. Are you ready to step into the responsibility of your new perspectives?

The truth of these messages will become clearer as you see the continuation of daily events to unfold. As time progresses, the controllers become less concerned with hiding the truth of their plans. The more they feel that victory for them is close, the more arrogant they will become. Soon, it will be more or less on open display and clearly 'in your faces.' As you observe these currents unfolding, you may wish to return to reread these volumes of messages – they shall become clearer to you. With each reading, a deeper understanding is reached, and a finer perception unfolds. The wisdom of these messages shall become clearer for you. It shall also become clear that it IS possible to transcend the current circumstances. A responsive enthusiasm for creating a new life experience upon this planet is itself a form of contagion. All contagions have their own ways and means of spreading. Some are air-born – others are thought-forms.

Significant opportunities are at hand for the evolvement of humankind. The time has arrived for each aware individual to stand in their own truth – and to embrace it. The time of crisis has arrived. Personal choices must be made. If anything, it is now time to turn to the personal realm where the inner foundation can be built strong. Within the collective human awareness resides each individual conscious contribution. The individual and collective reside within the same realm. The only difference is the pinpoint of focus. Each perceptual pinpoint of awareness brings its own dynamics into the whole. It is the 'connecting – linking' of these individual focuses of awareness that is now our focus here. Focus of awareness forms intentional thought. Intentional thought creates physical manifestation. The correspondences and relations of intentional thought is the roadmap for creating a new paradigm of life experience. Top-down movements usher in control. Bottom-up movements facilitate the energies of change.

Purposeful interactions are the dynamics that shall facilitate the required change within human life. These shall form the conscious flows that share not only information but also conscious awareness and intent. These flows exist within the field of potentiality in which holds physical manifestation. The potentials available within the 'field of potentiality' are limited only by the degree of *awareness of conscious access*. In truth, everything awaits 'in potential.' The missing link is the understanding of how to utilize this field of available energy. Each individual 'pinpoint of awareness' is also a mini-field within this collective field of potentiality. YOU each have your own space of potential energy within your personal sphere of influence. How to connect? Use your INTENT.

Your individual perceptual bubbles of awareness also align with other like-resonance – or like-awareness – groupings. These groupings form an energetic entrainment that increases their strength and power of focused intent. Consider this process:

Awareness – Connection – Resonance –

Those of you who have continued to read these messages to this point have done so because there is an original intention guiding your current life experience. And this original intention is aligned with the intent of these messages. In understanding this, it then follows that your intention, or purpose, is aligned with supporting and furthering the evolvement of humanity upon this planet. For this is also the intention of these messages. Synchronistic alignments occur for a reason. That reason is usually to participate in a shared purpose. Consider your life thus far. Has there not been a pattern of connections that could be said to be influenced by an underlying intention that guides your life? Some lives move more easily - in the 'flow' - if they are aligned, or in sync, with their underlying current of intentions. Aligning with one's individual intention in the personal realm helps to support the individual contribution for the collective. Operation: Human Freedom also requires that people recognize, accept, and then purposefully align with the current of their original intention. This then leads to a more dynamic and energetically-endowed purpose of intent. Each recognition and acceptance further strengthens the focus of energy. Some people walk through their life experience like a laser – others like a dim light. This is not a judgement but an observation.

The establishing of each person's foundation means coming into synchronization with their original intent. A person is then said to be more 'in flow' and in balance with their lives. This personal foundation is of great benefit to the larger network, or community, of like-awareness and resonance. A solid foundation allows a person to perceive more clearly through the distorted fog of reality.

A clear line of view through the distortion field is required.

The intention to pursue genuine human freedom does itself begin the processes of change. The thought-intention is enough to get the ball rolling. Your intent will draw contacts and circumstances to you that shall allow for the sharing of this information. It is good to be observant of such opportunities and situations. Assess each moment accordingly. Allow your presence to 'spread the word' by the correct placing of either information or focused and intentional energy. What may appear to be a small contribution may be part of larger consequences in the plan to liberate humanity from its perceptual prison. Never dismiss the potential that small contributions can make.

Acknowledgment and understanding of the subjugation of humankind is necessary for effective purposeful intent. Saying this, it is detrimental too if the focus remains on the negativity of the controlling agenda rather than on the desired change. There is a strong current of delusion that is persuading people that there is no alternative to the way things are going. That is, towards further containment and control of humanity. This persuasive delusion is part of the controller's agenda of programming and propaganda. Yet self-aware consciousness has far greater power. The power inherent within humanity's self-awareness has been deliberately hidden from public knowledge for thousands of years. You have been denied knowledge of your birthright. It is time to stop self-perpetuating the controlling agenda that is against you.

All power is energized by intention.
Focus your intention – utilize it.
Nothing can be purposefully achieved without intention.

There is no more 'going with the flow of the masses' unless a person prefers their ignorance and docility. To change the course of the controlling agenda now will entail a period of chaos. It will be necessary then to be prepared for this chaos. Within the chaos shall be the optimum time for communication of this information.

Your communication channels allow you to also share this information *anonymously,* if you so wish to do so.

TWENTY ONE

It would be beneficial for people to keep reminding themselves that what they see and hear in the mainstream news and information channels has been deliberately prepared for them. The programming is aimed to disempower the people – to make them feel powerless against the rising tide coming toward them. However bad the situation 'appears' to be is always a deliberate distortion. Do not measure your own capacities in relation to the false external programming. It would be an error to rely upon tangible resources when the greatest empowerment comes from an intangible realm.

The onslaught of dis- and mis-information will only increase. It is an attempt to overwhelm you. Their 'information' is also heavily loaded with emotionally manipulative content and energies. Its aim is to impact your emotional centers and to destabilize you. Observe these tactics and strategies but do not become entangled with them. Observe with conscious awareness. Your connection is with the creative flow that relates with a universal evolvement. Your conscious awareness should not be mudded by the dirt of the darker energies. These darker, obstructive forces aim to block the expansion of conscious awareness. This is a corrosive path that goes against the creative cosmic flow. Because of this, there is a bottleneck within this zone of the expansion of conscious awareness. The two sides of this bottleneck are now more visibly noticeable, and this visibility will increase. The arrogance of the controllers is getting to the point where they are less bothered in trying to hide their intentions. Soon it will become obvious that there is a position that people will need to make - and a decision to take. The lines are becoming more clearly drawn. Those reading now have most likely already made that decision. We would hope so.

It is time to consider whether these three volumes of messages have made any change, or shift, within the reader's own personal life and perspectives. If there has been a shift, then consider how much so this could occur on a larger, collective scale. What is within the individual also ripples out into the collective. And to keep in mind that the reality that human life is experiencing upon this planet is such because of a collective consensus agreement. Your consensual agreement has been manufactured and curated – far beyond your knowing and awareness. Consider what could happen if this agreement was taken back? This is not beyond the realm of possibility. The focus of intent needs to be kept upon conscious awareness and on your empowerment. Your individual and collective focus is being distracted and undermined. Do not accept this so easily. Take back your focus. Then align this focus with intent and purpose. You do not resist with fists but through re-tooling your purpose and aligning with your intention.

The controlling agenda is to get your compliance through a collective agreement to not disagree. There will always be those people who will physically resist and push back. The majority, however, will acquiesce through quiet compliance. We recommend neither complicity nor protest. Both these paths only serve to restate the incumbent status quo. Protesting against anything only reinforces the thing you are protesting. What we suggest is shifting the life experience by navigating to a new reality paradigm. The path to this objective is through aligning with the natural universal laws and with the evolving creative flow.

As we have outlined previously, consider carefully the attraction energetics of like-resonance; focused intent and purpose; and allowance. These drivers then align with harmony and balance. What is needed here is a great 'mind change' across the planet. This operation for human awareness and freedom has been in play for a great many of your years already. Now the moment is pivotal.

If every individual upon the planet chose to change their agreement upon the current reality, then it would literally dissolve overnight. Yet this is not going to happen – nor does it need to. Humanity is not a single pattern. Humanity is not a homogenous collective. There is nothing standardized about humanity. It is a wonderfully diverse and creative species. Only the false structures that have contained you have established the standardization and norms that now measure you. Individual consciousnesses were always meant to pursue their own paths of evolvement; and the wisdom and experience gained to be channeled into the collective as a positive enhancement. Now those channels of nutrition have become corrupted and the collective wisdom hungers.

Listen: do not take human subservience as a given. Human life is tenacious. It may seem fragile at times, yet the human species would not have arrived to where it is now without formidable resilience and persistence. You belong to a surviving species, not a redundant one. Your capacities are beyond your measurements. The containment and subservience of the human race is not an easy task by any means. Be proud of your toughness of spirit and resolute courage. The human species has shown its merit for further evolvement without question. Time now to show that steadfast valor and stubborn persistence like never before. The programming influence upon human consciousness has been dominant and persistent and still human consciousness continues to evolve. The only way for 'them' to contain an evolving humanity is through more brutal methods. For this, a new phase of containment and control is underway. This is a sign of the controllers' desperation; it is also a sign for humans to wake up, fast.

Give up the differences that
cause you dissonance.
Focus upon the similarities that
bring you resonance.
Do not slide further into divide but
energize the unity.

Allow now multiple intentions to operate within

your relations. We suggest you do not block, contest, or debate against other people's intentions but rather allow all. Even if you do not agree with someone, the blocking energy does more harm than is recognized. The energy of allowance is supporting of conscious awareness to seek its own relational paths. Accept the intentions of your fellow human beings even if you do not agree with them. Remember that all humans are humans *becoming*. Allow people to 'become' through their own paths of experience. Keep your energies unified and do not waste on matters that fuel division and difference.

The need or desire for a sense of security is likely to arise within people as they sense the external dissonances. Yet consider that external securities are likely to be false pillars that you become tied to. Real security is within yourselves, and the relations and connections you have with like-minded – or like-resonant – friends and contacts. Increase your relations with those of like-resonance rather than jumping into external structures. The path at this time is to fully human *become*. That is, it is a path toward the fully human being. Any path that lessens the independence of the full human being is a path supported by other ulterior motives. Operation: Human Freedom is walking the path toward the fully human being. This is the path of your inherent evolvement that resides within your species awaiting its full natural, biological unfoldment. You will clearly see other paths, other agendas, being offered and presented to you. They will seem tempting. We urge you to consider the question of human betterment. What does human *betterment* signify? Does it involve leaving the human behind?

You are HU-man. The HU breath of the Source flows through you. Do not give away your heritage so lightly.

Focus on expanding the human experience as you observe the chaos unfolding around you. Observe but do not become entangled in these dissonant energies. Stay focused. Stay with purposeful intent. Nothing can be manifested without relation to intention. You must live with the faith and trust of the intangible before it can, or will, become tangible to you. Trust in your own process. Trust in the larger process too. Place your trust on the side you have chosen. Do not think of this as a 'war.' If you think in terms of a war, then you shall attract war energies to you. Consider this as more of a *process of experience*. And allow this experience to become knowledge for you – and then finally for this knowledge to become wisdom.

Humanity is in the driving seat of its own chariot. Whilst the generalities of the emerging patterns can be known, the specifics of how events will unfold are related to what 'happens on the ground.' There are still many open variables, and places in the pattern where 'interventions' can occur at optimal times. Humans are unpredictable and, in this case, it is a highly advantageous trait for you. You have been chasing your own tails for too long now. If humanity continues to tail chase, then it shall become exhausted and slip into structures of servitude. Once the first puzzle pieces begin to fall into place, then the rest come quickly. Your intention now should be to place those first few pieces in order to allow a new pattern matrix to be established. After you set up this new pattern, other pieces will be attracted to this new resonance. Initially a slow start, the process then accelerates to an astonishing degree. Consider your life patterns - perhaps you have been placing those initial pieces all along? It has taken you your lifetime so far to have the first pieces of your puzzle in place. Now, you can observe how your pattern is attracting the new pieces. Observe how fast they are coming now and slotting into place.

Everything you have done
has brought you to this point.
This can be a simplistic phrase,
or it can hold great meaning.
Only you can know.
Only you can choose.

Get used to your choices.

TWENTY TWO

The conscious cosmos of which humanity is a part is there to help those people who first learn to help themselves. There is energetic assistance to those individuals who strive, with sincere intention, for the betterment of themselves and others. By working for this betterment, a person shows others their intention by action and participation. This never goes unnoticed. It only may not be noticed in the ways one expects. The individual consciousness that pushes against its limits also pushes others. By rising up the rung of the ladder, it allows others to rise also. It is the negative energy that pushes others down, into the cave of shadows.

Freedom is about not aligning with those people, plans, or energies that wish to limit the human life experience and the further expansion of consciousness. Encouragement and support toward the expansion of life is the natural evolvement of the universe. All those who are aligned with the intent of the universe are there to support others with the same intent of purpose. The 'bigger picture' unfolds as a person moves through their life experience putting together the pieces of the puzzle picture. So many people have the thought that – 'there must be more to life than this?' Yet few are the people who actually act upon this thought to unravel the maze around them. Few are the people who listen and follow the silent nudges within them. You are being messaged all the time. You are at home, but no-one is picking up the phone.

Freedom is also discovering the process that is discovering itself. Freedom is about learning *to see* what is freedom within the self. Conscious life is learning itself consciously.

Freedom of self comes naturally as a process of awareness consciously remembering and thus evolving. Any blockage on this growth of awareness is a constraint upon freedom. Awareness is the real target here. Control over this planet has been fostered because of the control placed over human awareness. Your freedom depends upon the many of you growing into your natural awareness. But YOU need to do the work. Don't expect to wake up one morning with a fresh dose of awareness.

As per the first universal law, you are to 'attract' those elements conducive to awakening into your life experience.

Freedom is also a state of consciousness. Consciousness is that which manifests through all physical beings. It is also what manifests through what you often call your 'mind.' Access to this consciousness has also been limited by a manipulated life experience on this planet. The consciousness that humans have access to is only a small slither of the potential consciousness that is available. That is why humans can neither perceive what their full freedom should be or what their current incarceration is. To perceive this situation in its truer form, people need to develop their access to consciousness. That is, to become more consciously aware. Again, we are back to the choices you each make. By striving for greater conscious awareness, you can attract those forces conducive to your aim. Yet you need to demonstrate your intent.

The reason that humanity finds itself in the situation it is in, is partly due to there not having been enough individuals seeking genuine freedom. We repeat the saying we gave in Volume 2:

'The bird which knows not of sweet water has his beak in salt water all the year'

Not having endeavored to strive, find, and taste genuine conscious freedom, the average human being is content with the life experience of non-freedom (salt water). This accounts for why people continue to put their dependence and trust in institutions and rituals that keep them 'stuck' and constrained. Humanity's evolvement has become stuck on a treadmill. You are all walking fast but making little forward movement. Your technologies have 'progressed' and yet your social conditions of poverty, starvation, inequality, etc., have not improved at a sufficient pace (to put it mildly). Humanity's material conditions have improved as a way to cover up the poverty that exists within you. The more you are pacified and pleased by the external toys, the less you are aware of the internal condition of humanity. The delusion is to distract you from the inner core – this is where your true power lies. The grand aim of the controllers is to be able to cut off humanity permanently from their inner core and hence from any remembrance of Source. If this ever happens, your species will be thrust into a void and your line of evolvement effectively curtailed – or stopped altogether. Freedom for the individual is also eventually freedom for the collective species.

Continuing down the current path will not bring a different outcome to your life experience. Many grand cycles are now coming to a completion. This is what makes this particular period a critical time. It is a 'breakthrough' or 'breakdown' moment, in your modern terms. Great choices have to be made now. Each individual now must make a decision on what type of future they wish for themselves, and for those people they can take along with them. Your 'grand institutions' will not help you. Neither your religions nor your sciences will provide you with the resources you require for reaching human freedom. Are you still prepared to play the waiting game? Do you feel you have time?

The way forward is to build a new foundation. A new foundation of thought, understanding, knowledge, and wisdom. A new foundation built on awareness and perception. A new foundation built on collecting together those individuals of like-resonance. Create your foundations within and around you. Time now to create and establish a new human life experience upon this planet. A time to step out of the darkness from where humanity has lingered too long.

There is an urgency now to these matters. Have you not felt the 'running away' of time? Does it not feel like it is accelerating away from you, and out of your hands? Staying on the treadmill, or paddling water, are no longer options. Staying still is a precursor to falling back. The only way is the way ahead. The only way is the way back home.

Operation: Human Freedom is about encouraging every individual - each reader here - to develop their own life experience by making the necessary changes to raise conscious awareness. Each individual change will ripple out into the collective. Help others to help themselves by first helping YOUR SELF. Use your discernment; gain knowledge through this discernment; turn this knowledge into wisdom - then find your own *knowing*. Once you have this 'knowing,' you will know what to do and how to act. You *just* will.

It is time to decide whether the life you currently lead is the life you wish to continue living. Is it the right path for you? Are YOU and your own freedom worth committing to?

It is time to leave the repetitive cycles. It is time to get off the running wheel of the rat's race. True life should be in perpetual, forward motion. Are you free in this movement? Are you committed to further movement? Greater restrictions will soon be upon you. It shall be important to develop connections and energetic flow between like-minded individuals. Create your networks. Find your 'family of like-resonance.'

Life circumstances may become more extreme in many areas. Focus on these circumstances as opportunities to trigger and stimulate greater awareness within yourself and within others. Assist others to *see* if they are open and willing for this. Do not waste energies upon those people, contacts, or networks that are not open to receive such information. Use the limited time to empower like-resonance connections. As chaotic energies and disruptions arise, it will be more important than ever to hold a 'stable space.' It shall be your responsibility to keep a 'good head' whilst others around you may be losing theirs. As in the past, all those 'aware individuals,' or groups, have maintained a refuge of resonant, harmonious energy as a sanctuary against the external dissonance. We suggest that YOU each become your own refuge and sanctuaries of conscious awareness. You will then become the beacons that will shine out over the outer dimness and this light will impact, affect, and attract others to the light.

Beacons are needed now. It is time to light up the inner fire.

The steadfastness of the few will compensate for the ignorance of the many. The thread that binds humanity to Source will never be severed as long as there are those who remember. For those who are aware, it is imperative now to not only maintain but further strengthen that awareness. Awareness itself is a wave of light. Choose how best to disseminate your resonant energies. Do not doubt that small actions and contributions will have their effect. Small actions can operate under the radar effectively. Many small actions make up a multitude.

Keep your mental and physical constitution strong and healthy. Freedom needs nutrients to feed its way. Freedom means *holding your center* whilst the storm rages. The center of the cyclone is where you each need to be. That center is within every one of you. Remember - atoms do not need to be touching to be joined together. And yet they create the strongest of structures. You may not physically know your fellow atoms, yet *you shall be known* by your vibration and resonance. Gain and align with the frequencies of freedom, and trust that you will be aligned with others upon the same frequencies.

Many vibrations synchronize to create a whole focus of intention. Even if it 'appears' that you are doing nothing, trust that by **being** you are contributing to the plan of Source. And it shall be better for you that it 'appears' that you are doing nothing so that the Machine does not take an interest in your presence. Your role, if you accept it, is to join with the **human becoming**.

There shall be a revolution in human becoming. Each atom will hold its center. Each shall encourage the *quiet ones* to play their part. Each individual contribution is important. Each and every alignment with the plan for human evolvement is crucial. Humility, stability, dignity, and courage in the human becoming will create the great waves of energetic alignment. Those who know the alternative, know that there is no alternative to freedom. Those who *know*, know that there is no choice but to choose Freedom. Having no choice in this shall allow you the greatest freedom from which to begin.

Freedom from the need for recognition in a world that thrives on attention will also bring you great freedom and a space to operate from. Service to freedom comes free from social recognition and gratification. Knowing this now will make it easier for you to step ahead.

Subtle steps shall make powerful waves. Tread softly in order to tread with the greatest purpose and intention. There are rocks in the road ahead, yet light feet will not be damaged. Stay close to the ground; stay close to the grass; stay close to the roots. Wherever you are, you are not alone. Trust in this. Trust in yourself. Trust in what you *feel* and *know* to be true.

There is a revolution coming. It will not come in the ways people expect. If you have arrived at this sentence, then it is likely you are already a part of it. Choose freedom by *holding the center* of Self.

Operation: Human Freedom exists because of YOU.
Each of you is a revolution in human becoming.
WE thank you.

Over to You.

ABOUT KSP

You are the atom, the wave, the whole.

You are the center.

You are FREEDOM.

You have a purpose.
USE it.

Kaleb Seth Perl

Made in the USA
Coppell, TX
03 April 2022

75966439R00104